modern gardens and the landscape

revised edition

by Elizabeth B. Kassler

The Museum of Modern Art, New York

acknowledgments

This book would not exist without Arthur Drexler, Director of the Museum's Department of Architecture and Design, who not only proposed it, but was generous with advice and encouragement during its preparation; and it is doubtful that he would have proposed it if I had not previously written about water for John Knox Shear, late editor of the *Architectural Record*.

Armando Salas Portugal's photographs of Barragán's work were obtained by Mildred Constantine, the Museum's Associate Director of Graphic Design, through the good offices of Max Cetto and Mathias Goeritz. Some of the material on Burle Marx came from Anthony Walmsley and Lota Macedo-Soares, on Denmark from Richard Cripps, on Sweden from Charles Agle; and Sven Selow produced the plan of the Forest Cemetery, photographed from Asplund's original drawing. George Barrows, of the Museum staff, helped collect American photographs, and Lawrence Perkins sent the pictures of Jensen's Columbus Park. I wish to thank all these people for their kindness, also those who at one time or another read and criticized the manuscript: Kenneth Kassler, Catherine and William Wurster, Clarinda and John Lincoln, Frederick Gutheim, Edgar Kaufmann, and the late Henry Churchill.

Beyond formal expression is the debt to George Rowley and to Frank Lloyd Wright, beloved teachers both now dead. From George Rowley, connoisseur of Chinese painting and Professor of Art and Archaeology at Princeton University, comes my conviction that man's relation to nature has a great deal to do with his art; from Frank Lloyd Wright comes my knowledge that the proposition works also in reverse—that art can give man a feeling that he is no stranger to the earth.

Elizabeth B. Kassler

Princeton, 1964

It is a pleasure to report that the passage of twenty years has diminished neither dear Arthur Drexler's editorial perspicacity nor the Museum's tolerance of my rather unconventional view of landscape design.

Special thanks on this round go to my niece, Sadie Wurster Super, who introduced me to the 1969 book on People's Park and went to great trouble to track down the photographer of the picture used here, also to Celia Scott Maxwell, who turned my attention to the Parc de la Villette competition and the late work of Carlo Scarpa.

Finally, I am deeply indebted to Princeton University's Library of Urban and Environmental Studies for almost fifty years of generous assistance and to the American Landscape Architecture Foundation for their suggestion to the Museum that a new edition of this book might be timely.

—E. B. K.

Princeton, 1984

FRONT COVER. Luis Barragán: Plaza del Companario, Las Arboledas, State of Mexico, 1960.

BACK COVER. Carlo Scarpa: Brion-Vega Cemetery, San Vito de Altivole, Treviso, Italy, 1970–72.

contents

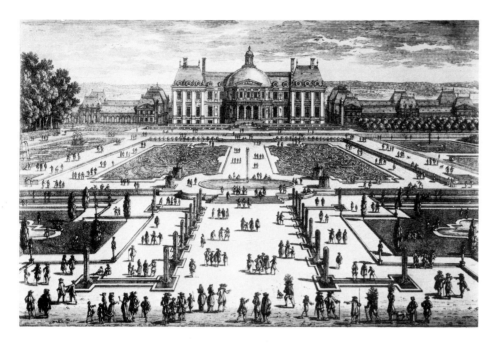

Gardens of Vaux-le-Vicomte, designed 1656–61 by André Le Nôtre, from a seventeenth-century engraving by Pérelle.
Nature played a subordinate, almost extraneous part.

Gardens of the Katsura Imperial Villa, Kyoto, Japan, c. 1636.
An unsentimental effort to penetrate to the essence of nature.

We are surrounded with things which we have not made and which have a life and structure different from our own: trees, flowers, grasses, rivers, hills, clouds. For centuries they have inspired us with curiosity and awe. They have been objects of delight. We have recreated them in our imaginations to reflect our moods. And we have come to think of them as contributing to an idea which we have called nature.

—*Kenneth Clark, 1949*

man and nature

When men have had a strong shared sense of their place in the universe, their gardens too have tended to be strong and sure, for the making of a garden is always something of an act of faith. If people of different times and places have had very different ideas of the way a garden should be organized, it is largely because they have made very different assumptions, strongly affecting their esthetic preferences, as to the relationship between man and nature.

Consider the Villa Lante and the Villa d'Este, Vaux-le-Vicomte and Versailles. Would these masterpieces of Renaissance and Baroque Europe have been possible had man not felt himself separate from and superior to the natural order? Nature played a subordinate, almost extraneous part in these gardens of the sixteenth and seventeenth centuries, for rational man, divorced from his biological context, acted in his Biblical role as lord of creation. Imposing his magnificent mathematics upon land and plants alike, he ordered the garden around his own triumphant progress down a straight central axis—an axis given special authority by its symmetrically balanced sides, and forced recalcitrant greenery into Euclid's ideal shapes. As formally geometric and architectural as the building of which it was the logical extension, the garden was man's triumph over nature. More than any other art form, it was direct expression of man's faith in himself as center of the universe.

The Chinese and the Japanese were given no divine assurance of dominion over the earth. For them man was part of universal nature, and no more particularly fashioned after the likeness of God than are the fish of the sea and the fowl of the air; no more than trees, flowers, grasses, rivers, hills, clouds; no more than rocks. Considering a garden, like a painted landscape, as an attempt to capture "the life-movement of the spirit through the rhythm of things," they sought to create a place where man would feel in harmony with cosmic forces, a place where the sense of otherness would give way to the sense of oneness. Design was not based on the abstractions of geometry, but on the artist's perception of the life-rhythms of nature and the inner relatedness of one thing to another—mountain to water, solid to void, active to passive. The garden was not organized along static man-centered axes, but with the same moving focus that brings the observer into a Chinese landscape painting as an active participant. Rather than an imposition of order from without, it was an unsentimental effort to penetrate to the essence of nature.

Today the certainties of the Renaissance and the certainties of the Far East seem equally remote. We share only our uncertainties. Progenitor and product of the industrial and scientific revolutions, modern man seems to feel neither above "nature" nor part of it, merely alien. To judge from contemporary writing and painting, we seem not too sure, inside, that it is anything more than an agglomeration of arbitrary fragments of experience. Cast in our own image is the cruel and meaningless dreariness of the man-altered environment, this creeping wasteland in which we have our being.

We are out of joint with nature, and out of joint with our own natures as a consequence. If this is the way it must be, then art and nature are best kept separate from each other. Scrupulous separation, even a wilfully shocking expression of disjointedness, would seem to be more real (and better art) than the application of extraneous harmonies to indifferent nature in a pious attempt to persuade ourselves that, though we are strangers to this earth, we are at least In Charge.

If, on the other hand, visible nature is not hopelessly and absurdly irrelevant to the human condition, if there is still a chance for us to find ourselves within a whole, perhaps landscape art can help us to a sense of meaningful relationship. A Western artist who feels that earth and trees and water do have possible relevance to man must create that relevance himself. Unlike a Chinese or Japanese, he works out of no common background of understanding, and has no familiar symbols to help him; yet it is possible, possible that he will in his own way make the nature of nature accessible to our awareness and to our sense of lively participation.

Outdoor room with fountain, from a seventeenth-century engraving by Venturini.
Planting can offer a spatial experience.

a frame of reference

Since the landscape designer's materials often come to hand already fashioned as objects of delight—either through their own life or through the impact of natural forces—his art may lie partly in omission: the ground may be spared the bulldozer, the stream flow free of channel or culvert, the woods avoid the chainsaw, and the shrub escape the clippers; but in so far as he is an artist, not merely a conservationist, he will one way or another shape his materials into fresh content. If only through addition or subtraction he will recreate nature.

The way in which he approaches the landscape today is affected, consciously or unconsciously, by many factors—some out of the present, others out of the past. Although a few contemporary designers deny all connection with history, to the lay observer similarities seem not always coincidental, and tradition not invariably dead.

The classical tradition: landscape design as architecture

The old gardens of China and Japan were the work of poets, painters, philosophers, but in our part of the world landscape art has generally been considered a form of architecture. In ancient Rome, in the Renaissance, and again in the late nineteenth and the twentieth centuries it has been men of architectural inclination, if not always with specific architectural training, who have dominated the art; and in the United States, ever since the curriculum was introduced late in the nineteenth century, the professional designer is almost invariably a graduate "landscape architect," or an architect who feels that buildings and settings are one problem rather than two.

Association of the two arts makes a great deal of sense. Both are environmental arts, concerned with the impact of man upon his surroundings and with the impact of his surroundings upon man, and seeking their ends through the integration of use with beauty. Both serve man's convenience and comfort, whether indoors or out, therefore share certain fundamental techniques of planning and construction; and both serve man's pleasure by providing a continuous experience of changing relationships, synchronous with his own body's movement in space and time. Both professions look beyond the individual building, the individual garden, to the great problems of urban design and regional development, for theirs are social arts, affecting the lives of all manner of people by bringing them into new and potentially fruitful relationships with each other and with the world about them.

Since architecture implies a rational ordering of plan and construction, gardens laid out with T-square, triangle, and compass, are generally called architectural. Nevertheless, as Laotse intimated long ago, the reality of architecture lies neither in its materials nor in its geometry, but in its space; and only a garden that offers a vivid experience of space in its three full dimensions is in this sense of the word architectural. Whether forms be geometric or free is unimportant. What does matter is the presence or absence of a suggestion of bodily containment.

As every amateur of cities knows, space can be shaped outdoors as well as in, and the open areas between buildings are on occasion more positive than the buildings themselves. (Few people would exchange St. Mark's Square in Venice for any of the buildings that define it.) When height and breadth and depth all work together, planting can offer a spatial experience without help from man-made walls and ceiling. Canopies of branches can suggest scale and shelter even as their high shifting patterns evoke a relationship with the sky. Supporting trunks are structural columns, while shrubs and low-branching trees, whether left in their natural exuberance or clipped into flat textured planes, become defining walls of any desired height. Planting lends itself to almost any kind of spatial elaboration, any subtlety of perspective, any degree of formality, any decorative effect. Beneath is the ground, itself a plastic element that can be raised or lowered, tilted or leveled, terraced or contoured, to mold a flow of space. As flat sheets or serried jets, water too can define space and, through reflection or penetration, relate to the sky. As though that weren't enough, it offers itself as animated ornament.

There is a point, however, at which the easy parallel between the two arts becomes inadequate. Can lumber really be equated with a living tree? Is there not a profound difference in kind between the docile materials stacked in a building-supply yard and the irregular, unabstracted, intractable, yet lawful materials of animate nature? Is the ground, the surface of the earth, a passive medium without possible claims of its own? And water, protean water, can it be classed with any finality as an architectural material? The identification of outdoor space with architectural space is also a half-truth, for the sky is not a blue vault but an endless void.

Over-insistence on landscape art as planning and building and space creation can have unfortunate consequences, aggravated in this day of "personality cult" architecture. It promotes irrelevant geometry, and easily turns formality into formalism. It encourages the designer to assert himself where he might wisely be quiet and fosters, among those of lesser talent, a busy kind of showmanship that is distasteful in buildings and repellent when applied to the vast impersonal truths of nature. Worst of all, it discourages the designer from approaching his natural materials with the deep perception that can come only from profound understanding together with a certain degree of humility.

Because of the extraordinary character of these special materials, landscape art has a possibility that lies beyond architecture. It can offer an experience of architecture. It can also offer, with or without the assistance of architecture, an experience of universal nature.

Perhaps fortunately, the Western tradition is two-fold. If we inherit the ambiguous Renaissance concept of landscape art as architecture, we are also direct heirs to the non-geometric, anti-architectural "landscape style" invented by eighteenth-century English gentlemen for their rural seats. Whether adapted from the Italians, the French, or the Dutch, the formal garden had never rested easily on the open, undulating countryside of England, nor had its authoritarian bias suited the national psyche. It was inevitable that the English should stir from this Procrustean bed and not astounding, considering their strong attachment to their land, that in so doing they should make one of their few great contributions to the visual arts.

Almost from one generation to the next, and well before the articulate sensibilities of Romantic poetry, the English discovered nature. They found it habitable. Their taste for it extended even to wilderness: mountain and forest, desert and ocean, previously feared and avoided, were now relished as "sublime." Suddenly impatient with the rationalized artifice of wall and terrace, fountain, topiary, quincunx, and clipped avenue, they redesigned their ancestral gardens with seventeenth-century landscape painting as model, particularly the gently ideal-

Claude Lorrain (1600–1682): Landscape with a Piping Shepherd.

Blenheim Palace, Oxfordshire. Palace (1705) and Palladian bridge (1720) by Sir John Vanbrugh. Remodeled park and artificial pond by Lancelot (Capability) Brown in early 1760s.
Art was evident . . . only in the perfect beauty of the scenery.

Prior Park, near Bath. Grounds and Palladian bridge possibly designed by Capability Brown in early 1760s.
Rough-cropped undulating meadows.

ized country scenes of Claude, and brought rough-cropped undulating meadows up to the very windows of their elegant mansions. The newly naturalized "landscape gardens," perhaps better called parks, were composed with a painter's eye for asymmetrical balance in depth, unity of character, harmony of color, and effects of light and shade; yet art was evident—theoretically, at least—only in the perfect beauty of the scenery. The designer would often be the owner himself; or he might be a painter (William Kent), or a professional gardener (Capability Brown), or a "country gentleman" (Humphrey Repton). Rarely would he be an architect. No matter what the professions, or lack of profession, of the designers, the beauty of the English countryside today is largely due to the consummate artistry, artfully concealed, with which they worked.

The landscape style is less a style than a live tradition. Popularized in the United States by Andrew Jackson Downing in the 1840s, it has been responsible for large metropolitan parks all over the world ever since Calvert Vaux and the great Frederick Law Olmsted designed New York's Central Park in 1858; and from Downing through Skidmore, Owings & Merrill it has been welcomed as a flexible basis for design wherever grounds are spacious and use not prohibitively intensive. Less specifically, it is the ancestor of the continuous tree-studded lawn that lines our pleasantest suburban streets, and provides the indispensable *tapis vert* upon which Le Corbusier poses the huge apartment slabs of his proposed cities.

Yet the idea of designing a landscape as a seventeenth-century painter might have composed it on his canvas has limited vitality today. If we are painters, we are twentieth-century painters, and anyway the comparison presumes a static

Grounds of Scotney Castle, Kent, designed c. 1837. The picturesque approach to landscape gardening, wilder and rougher than Brown's style.
Consummate artistry, artfully concealed.

Attributed to Ma Lin, Sung dynasty.
Chinese painters found the essence of a tree in its rhythmic structure.

quality in nature and in our relations with our environment that is foreign to our feeling in the matter. We feel uneasy, too, with the generalizing, idealizing function of the landscape style, and find a hint of the Dresden shepherdess in Capability Brown's idyllic pastures.

The present importance of the style, then, lies less in the timeless serenity of its typical compositions than in an invigorating principle that stands behind them, yet transcends them. It was Alexander Pope who in 1731 urged garden designers to

> Consult the Genius of the Place in all;
> That tells the Waters or to rise, or fall;
> Or helps th'ambitious Hill the heavens to scale,
> Or scoops in circling theatres the Vale;
> Calls in the Country, catches op'ning glades,
> Joins willing woods, and varies shades from shades;
> Now breaks, or now directs, th'intending Lines;
> Paints as you plant, and, as you work, designs.

Pope's own genius lay in his original interpretation of *genius loci*, which had referred to the minor mythical deity presiding at any particular location. In its new meaning as the individual character of a site and the artist's primary source of inspiration was implied a new—or newly conscious—attitude toward design.

"Consult the genius of the place in all." The principle is as pertinent to the problems of the twentieth century as it was two hundred years ago to the remodeling of a great landed estate. It requires neither lush, unspoiled country as start nor naturalistic design as means. Even a formal garden, even an urban plaza, even a building or an entire city can be informed by the spirit of its place. It can belong.

Influence from China and Japan

Respect for the natural beauty of plants we inherit from the English, but for the particular way in which we see them today we are more indebted to the Far East—to Chinese landscape painting as well as to Japanese gardens.

Western painters have liked to paint trees in the enveloping growth of high summer, when form becomes light-dappled mass, but Chinese painters found the essence of a tree in its rhythmic structure. Here they saw Tao, the Way of the Universe and "mother of all things under heaven." They delighted in the subtle life-movement of bamboo and the sinewed force of gnarled pines, and they painted the flowering plum in earliest spring, before leaves came to blur the jagged continuity of its bones. Japanese gardeners, in the work we most value, took a similar approach, choosing plants more for individuality of structure than for flowers or foliage, then pruning and training to intensify inherent rhythm.

Sand garden, Ryōanji Temple, near Kyoto, 1499.
A marvelous liveliness in the interactions of these very positive shapes.

Admiration for Oriental art has sharpened our awareness of plants as animate sculpture shaped by the interaction of growth and environment. Rocks too we can now see as sculpture, whether the single monumental stone or the artfully natural group, and through the influence of Japan we become newly alert to texture—of leaves, of rocks, of ground surfaces.

We like Japanese gardens. We like the economy of means that intensifies the life of each plant, the character of each rock, and we find a marvelous liveliness in the interactions of these very positive shapes. We like that preference for subtle suggestion over bald statement which makes the tenth contemplation of Ryōanji more profoundly satisfactory than the first. Sometimes, it is true, we see trees and shrubs as brutally deformed as they ever were by European geometry; occasionally the gardens seem to us contrived and precious; often they seem spatially inconclusive; yet they are by and large so much to our taste that there is a strong temptation to copy. For us, however, a landscape is not "mountain-water" as it has been to the Chinese and the Japanese. For us there has been neither Yang nor Yin, and no Tao to illuminate trees and rocks and grasses with spirit. Let us take, gratefully, only what we can make our own.

The Moslem contribution

From another exotic tradition, the Moslem, we are learning to develop new sensibilities and pursue new possibilities. Here the stimulus is simple and single: water, shaped for use and pleasure at many levels of experience.

This was living sounding water, frothing down carved chutes, leaping into jets, brimming over placid reflecting pools, and flowing through precisely cut stone channels to irrigate the garden and to connect one part with another, indoors with outdoors. Emphasis was always upon the water itself rather than, as in Europe, upon elaborate stonework and statuary; yet treatment was never nat-

A carved marble chute as source of water in a seventeenth-century Moslem garden at Aurangabad, India.

Persian summer pavilion with pool and channel, from an engraving in Flandin and Coste, *Voyage en Perse*, 1841.
Emphasis was always upon the water itself.

uralistic, for everything was shaped to reflect man's joy that water had been made available to the garden through his own ingenious intercession.

The same waterworks that brought life to the plants, structure and animation to the garden, and varied delight to the ear, were planned to mitigate the discomforts of a hot, dry climate. If we now talk of building in relation to climate, we enter a field in which the Moslem long ago proved himself expert.

Pressures of our own time

Against this background of inheritance and appropriation, pressures from within his own age affect the way in which today's landscape designer understands his art.

One way or another he is affected by the sweep of social change. Rich private clients give way to municipalities, park commissions, highway authorities, institutions, business enterprises, occasional small householders, and a stimulating new set of problems; the passing of the old-fashioned gardener brings a demand for easy maintenance through preservation of wild growth, reduction and simplification of lawn areas, avoidance of clipped hedges, limitation of flower beds; and the massive new interest in outdoor activity, encouraged by increased leisure, is a growing challenge.

The new age has brought no important new materials to the landscape artist. His basic mediums are still earth, water, masonry, and green growing things. It does, however, offer new techniques to facilitate earth-moving, whether for view, privacy, convenience, or simply for the beauty of the sculptured shapes. Sometimes the earth comes free as waste from depressed expressways, tunnels, or base-

Contour strip cropping and terracing on an irrigated farm in Texas. *An experience . . . extracted from natural land form.*

ment excavations. A bulldozer can devastate a landscape; on the other hand, it can—or rather, might—be used to offer an experience as intensely extracted from natural land form as the field-terraced mountains in certain parts of Southeast Asia or the contour-plowed fields of our own countryside.

A by-product of modern industrial society is the eagerness to escape from mechanized, regimented living. More than ever man relishes the feel of earth under his feet. More than ever he delights in spontaneity and freedom and wildness and irrationality, and where can he better look for this than to the landscape? The need is not wholly satisfied by holiday excursions. It makes demands on daily surroundings and even affects formal landscape architecture. The Grand Manner of Le Nôtre becomes foreign to us, and we are wary of axial symmetry even at the man-scale of Italian humanism. Outside, as inside, we prefer a freer, less presumptuous shaping, and favor an organization by which design elements are so dynamically interrelated that the separate identity of each one is enhanced, voids become positive forces, and man himself enters the composition more actively than in the classical tradition of bilateral or central symmetry. Independent, in this case, of important influence from the Orient, we nevertheless begin to approximate the Oriental insistence upon relatedness, rhythmic sequence, and the equilibrium of strong tensions. We do this in our own way, retaining much of our innate interest in direction, progress, climax.

When the element of formal design is a living plant, the preservation and enhancement of its separate identity is something of a problem. Geometrically clipped hedges, for instance, are as handsome as ever, and as useful in defining space. Some are illustrated in these pages. Yet hedges begin to look as quaint as topiary, simply because the imposition of geometry upon natural growth denies the plant its freedom and individuality. The future seems to belong to the artist who neither nullifies nor changes the character of his plant materials, but rather reveals their innermost idea. Often that idea is better expressed by groups or masses of like plants than by the single specimen or the motley assortment. Just as "a crowd, a host of golden daffodils" conveys the essence of daffodilness, so a grove of birch or beech or hemlock may provide a more intense experience than the single tree. Massing some varieties and using others as strong individuals, the designer can make such active relationships between his plants that their uniqueness is accentuated.

It becomes apparent that the architecture of the landscape, perhaps even more than the architecture of buildings, can be wholly ours—yet wholly free—only when structure and space are developed, in Frank Lloyd Wright's phrase, "out of the nature of materials." We demand a close relationship between indoors and outdoors, but wish the landscape to be itself, not an architectural appendage.

If a landscape is to be or become itself, it must be understood through every interpretive instrument. It must be understood through the ancient intuitions of sight and smell, touch and hearing, and through that sense by which we feel a place not as a static fact, but as a phenomenon joining past to future, time to eternity; through the shiny new tools of science; and through the bird's-eye view of flight—flying has changed the way we see and feel. Even with our feet firmly on the ground, awareness of the down-view expands head-on evidence. Just as we know that scale and position are relative and multiple, so we know from flight and from high-speed surface travel that the earth is endlessly round, and that a hillside in Connecticut is no limited parcel of land, but part of the vast continuum of the earth's surface—an habitat uneasily shared by man and nature, at present to the detriment of both.

As it becomes obvious that we have applied ourselves with more whim than wisdom to the critical problem of how best to live upon this earth, or rather, with this earth, we begin to realize that the work of fitting people to the land, and fitting the land to people, must be undertaken with much the same care for action and interaction that a forester might apply to his far simpler problems of ecology. And since a measure of beauty seems the happy by-product of any ecologically sound approach to land use, it is unlikely that our physical environment will be ugly if it is planned to respect both the nature of man and the nature of nature.

Should less be demanded of landscape design as an art than as a science? Isn't it possible that a garden or plaza or park or boulevard must finally be judged as an essay in the tenancy of the earth? If it is to pass such a test (and some of the work shown in this book would gracefully fail), it must look and feel ecologically valid. It must appear to be of its place, not on its place, and its natural materials must seem to belong together with a more than formal relationship.

Out of all this the artist makes his own truth. Like his brothers back through history to the mythical Garden, he will recreate the landscape according to his own subjective image of reality. As he takes hold of earth, plants, and water, the materials unique to his art, let him only beware lest he destroy through his act of possession the genius of that which he has sought to possess.

the outdoor room

Introverted, secluded, contained against the wilderness, the outdoor room is the archetypal garden. Even when gardens could safely embrace the far horizon, the amenities of enclosure were never entirely forgotten.

To be felt as a roofless room, a walled garden must be limited in area. The prototype is the inner court—the garden within the house rather than the house within the garden. The concept is traditional in Spanish America, but only in the last decade important in contemporary architecture. Our national distrust of property-line walls as undemocratic contributes to the present popularity of court houses, for the open-air privacy that cannot politely be provided outside the house is provided within. Some day a private outdoor room will be considered as indispensable to a dwelling as a bathroom.

As the courtyard principle is extended to row houses and apartments, schools and office buildings, architecture turns in upon itself with a new sense of space.

Since the natural landscape, though held in memory, may be unseen or barely glimpsed, the design of an outdoor room is remarkably free. Often it is furnished to contrast with the outer world: in a desert, it may be a jungle, but in a jungle it may be an oasis of austerity. Design will often be geometric, for within walls a geometric layout can seem as appropriate as it can seem inappropriate in open country. If surrounding walls are glass, the sense of enclosure dwindles. If they are patterned with doors and windows and sunshades, planting quickly looks fussy and quiet pools multiply the busy façades into dizziness. It is beautiful blank walls that best contain a garden court.

Rather than centering or adjoining a building, the closed garden can stand free in the landscape. The garden of a medieval castle was often a detached retreat, and Washington's visits to his high-walled flower and kitchen gardens at Mount Vernon also required a purposeful effort. Louis XIV and his courtiers walked far to reach salons and theaters carved out of the Versailles greenery. Isn't difficulty of attainment often conducive to increased enjoyment?

The reality of an outdoor room is finally the sky. No one has understood this better than Le Corbusier. Even when his roof gardens are entirely unplanted, as is often the case, they offer an intense experience of nature through their powerful relationship to sky and sun.

Bernard Rudofsky: Arnstein house, São Paulo, Brazil, 1941.
Indoor and outdoor rooms are enclosed by the same high wall, an austere background for free and luxuriant planting. Glimpsed beyond the orchid-hung trellis of the living-room court is the courtyard that adjoins the master bedroom, and the far door enters a third garden.

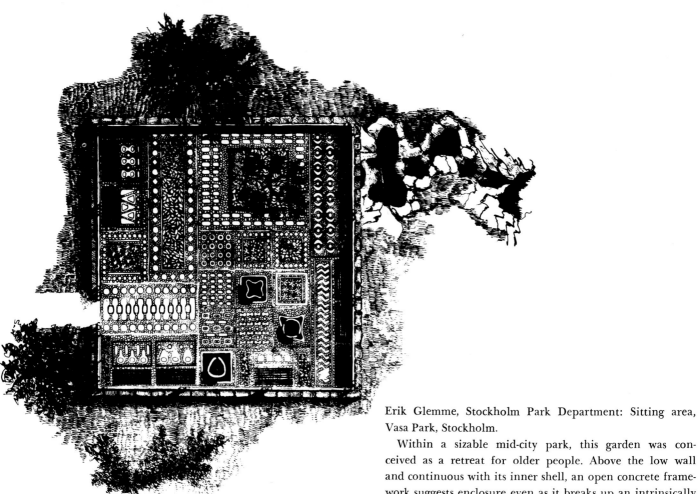

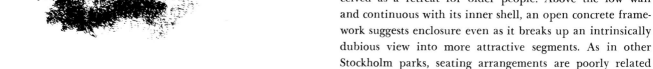

Erik Glemme, Stockholm Park Department: Sitting area, Vasa Park, Stockholm.

Within a sizable mid-city park, this garden was conceived as a retreat for older people. Above the low wall and continuous with its inner shell, an open concrete framework suggests enclosure even as it breaks up an intrinsically dubious view into more attractive segments. As in other Stockholm parks, seating arrangements are poorly related to the design.

Chief source of delight is the intricate pavement of pale gray stone slabs and dark gray cobbles set in concrete. Patterned of squares and oblongs, and put together with considerable freedom, it is less mechanical than the strict modular grid that is presently fashionable. Dwarf rhododendrons fill one of the raised planting boxes. Others are massed with flowers, changed with the seasons. One square frame is set below the pavement to contain a shallow pool and a thin jet of water.

Le Corbusier: Villa Savoye, Poissy-sur-Seine, France, 1930.

Enclosing the second-floor terrace is a prototype of the Vasa Park space-defining framework.

the outdoor room

Skidmore, Owings & Merrill: Reynolds Metals Company, Richmond, Virginia, 1958.

Based on the distance between supporting columns, the module of the courtyard floor relates outdoor space as closely to structure as indoor space. Some squares are set with red brick, some with grass, one with water. Dense masses of magnolia and holly appear to advantage against the patterned walls.

Skidmore, Owings & Merrill, architects; Sasaki, Walker & Associates, landscape consultants: The Upjohn Company, Kalamazoo, Michigan, 1961.

Of the nine inner courtyards that puncture the vast square building (see page 74), the entrance court illustrated at lower left is the largest and deepest. There are three distinct floor planes: the peripheral walk of gray granite, the lowered white marble paving of the garden area, and the great sheet of water that appears to flow from beneath the marble.

Shown directly below is one of the smaller courts. The vocabulary is similar, but broad architectural lines give way to smaller elements and an Oriental use of rocks and low evergreens.

Sutemi Horiguchi: Okada house and garden, Tokyo, 1933.

Designed by a student of Walter Gropius who became a pioneer of modern architecture in Japan, the garden is his personal synthesis of contemporary German ideas and the native classical tradition of the early Edo period.

Walls, terraces, and pool are an interplay of flat rectangular planes. Sharply defined against these noncommittal surfaces are isolated shapes of organic and inorganic nature, their separate identities strengthened by the tensions between them. Voids are as important as solids.

the outdoor room

Le Corbusier: Penthouse for Charles de Beistegui, Paris, 1931.

The experience was sky and sun rather than white walls and green grass carpet. The juxtaposition of fireplace and Arc de Triomphe was a witticism that served, in a way, to relate this now demolished roof garden to its locale.

Le Corbusier: Villa Savoye, Poissy-sur-Seine, France, 1930.

Even in the country Le Corbusier will often hoist outdoor living to the rooftops, for a garden or terrace at ground level blurs the rigorously clean distinction between man-made and natural forms that is basic to his art. The *toit jardin*, he feels, reclaims for use the outdoor area lost to construction and removes people from traffic and noise.

Divorced from the ground, his architecture often marries the sky. Even in his boxy buildings there are often powerful shapes that erupt through the roof and jab up into the void as though the forces behind them were too strong for polite containment. Sometimes these shapes suggest outdoor rooms.

Le Corbusier: Apartment house at Marseilles, France, 1952.

As the elemental power of Le Corbusier's architecture increases in later work, magnificent tensions are set up between buildings and distant horizon.

The relationship between the rugged mountains and the bold shapes of this rooftop playground is no accident. The mountains are abstracted in the inclined wall planes, and their actuality is brought into the composition by the changing perspectives of recessive columns that define foreground, middle ground, and distance.

the outdoor room

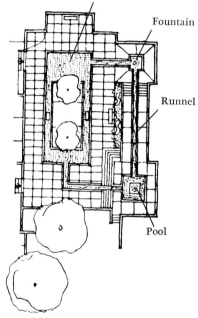

Pool

Fountain

Runnel

Pool

Lawrence Halprin: McIntyre garden, Hillsborough, California, 1961.

A series of outdoor rooms set into a California hillside, this Moslem water garden is almost as successfully naturalized as the Australian eucalypti that tower above it.

Emphasis is entirely upon the many faces, the many voices of water as it erupts in jets thick and thin, tumbles into basins, ripples through precisely cut stone channels, cascades down steps, burbles against interference, and comes to rest in a quiet pool.

The retaining wall steps down to affirm the slope of the land, avoiding awkwardness by changing direction at each change of level. More important than the walls is the floor, especially the insistent line of the smooth concrete edgings, reiterated in the broad horizontals of the stairs.

24

the outdoor room

Edward D. Stone: United States Embassy, New Delhi, India, 1958.

Offices open from a central water garden dappled with shadow by the gold-colored aluminum sunscreen that shelters it. Islands and stepping stones are asymmetrically disposed, and cantilevered edges make them seem to hover weightlessly over the water. In the Moslem tradition of northern India, jets are simple and single, issuing from inconspicuous nozzles.

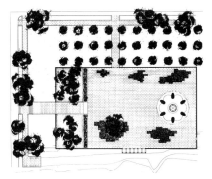

Philip Johnson: Roofless Church, New Harmony, Indiana, 1960.

Its name prompted by George Sand's remark that only the sky is a roof vast enough to embrace all worshipping humanity, the walled garden is used for non-denominational services in a Utopian community rich with mementos of Harmonists and Owenites.

The main entrance is through gates into a formal vestibule defined by a clipped hedge. Beyond, under a powerfully shaped canopy, is a Lipchitz bronze symbolizing the descent of the Holy Spirit. Symmetrical planting would have been the conventional adjunct to the strong central axis, dominated by the shrine. Instead the architect has made an active relationship between the folded, wood-shingled canopy, the sumptuous golden rain tree, and low masses of Burford holly, myrtle, and red geraniums. Planting beds defer to the right angles of the pavement, but without apparent loss of freedom.

the outdoor room

Holger Blom, Stockholm Park Department: Kungsträdgarden, Stockholm, c. 1955.

A small midtown plaza, originally laid out in the naturalistic landscape style, has been remodeled to this more useful and urbane design. Grass and paths were replaced by pavement inset with rectangular pools, informally massed flowers, and changing craft exhibits housed in elegant glass cases.

parks and plazas

Ever since Central Park was laid out in 1858 the landscape style has provided appropriate answers for large metropolitan parks, where naturalized greenery has a fair chance to look natural; but fragile grass set with picturesquely grouped trees is irrelevant to a small, intensively used plaza.

Often it is the ardent nature-lover who is most insistent on drawing a firm line between town and country. Let country be country, he says, and let town be town, and let an urban square be urbane—for, he might add, urbanity is the spirit of its place. And he will look for inspiration, if anywhere, to the elegance of Le Nôtre's Tuileries Gardens, or to the irregular, unplanted piazzas of medieval Italy, or to the variously delightful solutions of present-day Stockholm. He may or may not consider urban open space as architecture; but he will certainly treat it as landscape, not merely because it uses plant materials, which it may not do at all, but because it must make its peace with sun and sky, wind and rain, and because it belongs to the continuous surface of the earth. Not for him, the ruthless leveling of San Francisco's tilted squares for subterranean parking.

Plazas need people for completion. To ensure their free movement, restrictive paths defer to large areas of pavement, but pavement of such color, texture, and pattern that it serves as antidote to the asphalt jungle rather than continuation. Water too plays a major role, for people like to linger by festive waters even when their duties lie elsewhere. In some climates the legendary association of fire and water may offer possibilities. As one Victorian remarked, "A large chafing dish, containing a good fire, would be a far more agreeable ornament in the center of an English place or square, for at least eight months of the year, than any fountain."

In both city and suburb the isolated, neatly bounded park begins to give way to a continuous system of greenways, dedicated to pedestrians and bicyclists, that connect dwellings with schools and centers, broaden out here and there as gardens and playgrounds, and finally emerge into open country as rights of way through fields and woodland. Walking may again become a pleasure, perhaps with some attendant mitigation of the traffic problem.

Even at the vast scale of the metropolitan region, the shape of open areas can be as important in the visual image as the shape of urban areas. The "Year 2000" plan for our national capital, providing great wedges of open land between densely developed radial corridors, is an impressive effort in this direction.

Gunnar Asplund: Library Park, Stockholm, 1927–35.
From the right an artfully rustic stream tumbles down through boulders to the pond. Sculptured figures by Ivar Johnsson mark the fall of water into the great formal basin.

Flower parterre, Tivoli Gardens, Copenhagen.

As many travelers know, mid-city Tivoli offers all manner of delight: restaurants for every purse and concerts for every taste; zoo, playgrounds, and amusement park; boating ponds, water spectacles, and gardens that include the tranquil retreat illustrated here.

Within the free curves of a brick retaining wall (1) and a pond (3), the rhythmic arrangement of bubbling basins (2) and diagonal brick walks brings together low, immensely colorful plants and a scattering of trees.

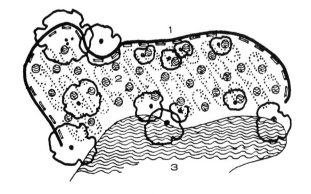

Sven Markelius and Holger Blom: Plaza at Vällingby, Stockholm.

The town square of Vällingby, a satellite of Stockholm, is unplanted. Hospitable to the northern sun and to citizens of every age, it offers circle-patterned granite paving and raised pools confined by circular benches.

Typical Stockholm street corner.

Holger Blom, the architect who headed the Stockholm Park Department, early in the 1930s designed reinforced concrete flower pots to group about the city as "portable gardens." Municipalities in other countries followed the Swedish example, though rarely with such success.

parks and plazas

Le Corbusier: Park of the capital of the Punjab, Chandigarh, India. Begun 1952.

The architect's sketch of 1952 shows the center of the huge park as a giant earth sculpture, with pools on two levels and massive staircases descending to sunken plazas. At the top of the drawing is the Governor's Palace, (1) on the photograph of the model. The Parliament (2) and the Secretariat (3) are out of view at left, while the Court of Justice (4) lies off at the right.

Le Corbusier uses artificial hills (5) and serried trees to obliterate unwanted views, to tie together the widely separated buildings, and to suggest scale in the vastness. The free-form mounds, piled up of earth excavated from the depressed highways and planted with an informal mixture of trees, play against the powerful geometry of the architecture; and walls of trees, arranged to form *"chambres de verdure,"* will occasionally close the horizon. Tree-wall and mound are sketched with the Secretariat at the foot of the page.

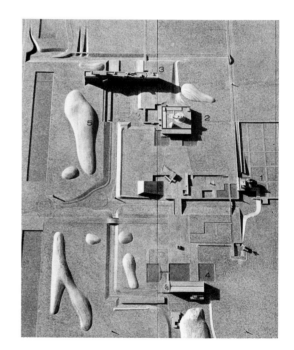

LEFT. Luis Barragán: Plaza del Bebedero de los Caballos (Plaza of the Horse Trough), in the subdivision of Las Arboledas, State of Mexico, 1958–62.

Barragán gives new meaning to the Mexican tradition of emphatic walls and strong color.

Towering eucalyptus trees are mirrored, silhouetted, and shadowed on flat planes of water, wall, and earth. Persians would have admired the economy of means and the emphasis upon water; and they would have claimed as their own the raised brimful pool with its narrow drip gutter—an ancient Persian device for extending reality into its reflected image. The long basin is literally a horse trough, for the plaza was conceived as a meeting place for riders.

Luis Barragán: Plaza del Campanario, Las Arboledas, State of Mexico, 1960.
(Illustrated in color on the front cover.)

Behind the sapling palisade is the eucalyptus avenue which leads to the Plaza del Bebedero, shown opposite.

[A visit three years ago to Las Arboledas, a not easily located residential subdivision northwest of Mexico City, found these masterworks neglected, vandalized, and doomed to follow El Pedregal into ruin unless preservation measures are quickly adopted. Since the public has access to only one other major Barragán fountain, the 1963–64 Fuente de Los Clubes, the loss of those at Las Arboledas would be catastrophic.—E.B.K., 1984]

Luis Barragán: Public fountain, Pedregal Gardens, Mexico, D.F., 1949.

Staggered lava walls complement a brimming pool, and water enters from an unexpected source.

parks and plazas

Luis Barragán: Plaza de las Fuentes (Plaza of the Fountains) in the subdivision of Pedregal Gardens, Mexico, D.F., 1951.

Laid up of indigenous purplish-black lava rock, walls play against each other to define a square pool, guarded by blue-painted iron pickets. The formal architectural framework emphasizes the dynamism of giant boulders, leaping water, and hoary eucalypti. The impingement of tree trunks upon pavement (of nature upon reason?), evidently important in the architect's intention, has something of the threat of pre-Columbian art.

It was Barragán's masterful use of walls that made this plaza memorable to early visitors. Now the little plaza seems insignificant, overpowered as it is by the clamor of surrounding houses, waterworks, and planting.

LEFT. Carl Milles: Milles Garden, Lidingö Island, near Stockholm.

Sculpture is brought together with sky and water in this terraced garden—once the private pleasure ground of the sculptor, but now open to the public. Emphasis here is less on the figures than on the abstract forest of pedestals that repeats the strong verticals of smokestacks on the far bank.

RIGHT. Roberto Burle Marx: Museum of Modern Art Plaza, Rio de Janeiro, 1955–61.

Stone walks define rectangular beds of such boldly differentiated character that the pattern and texture of this sunken garden can be read not only from the peripheral sidewalk, but from upper floors of distant office buildings. Planting is kept low to free the view of bay and mountains, and the mat of feathery, wind-tossed grass accentuates the character of rugged granite blocks and shiny, spiky leaves.

LEFT. Herbert Bayer: The Marble Garden, Aspen Meadows Hotel, Aspen, Colorado, 1955.

Slabs and blocks of unpolished white marble, found in an abandoned quarry near Aspen, were disposed on a thirty-six-foot-square platform to create interesting spatial relationships enlivened by strong shifting shadows and one tall jet. Sculpture to walk through, the garden stands free in an undulating meadow.

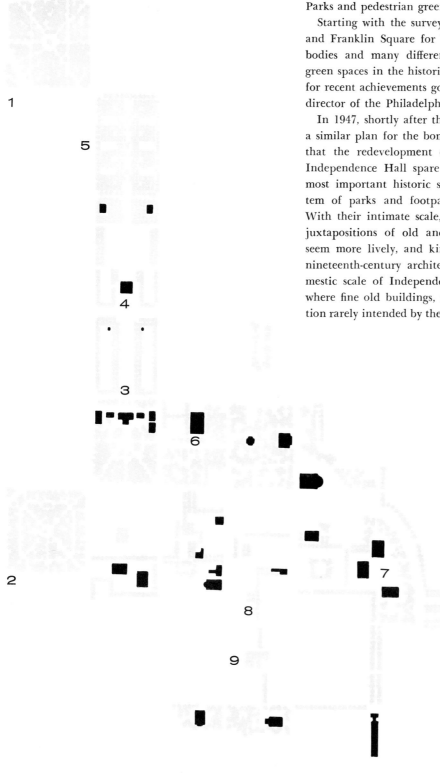

Parks and pedestrian greenways, east-central Philadelphia, 1947–75.

Starting with the surveyor who in 1683 laid out Washington Square and Franklin Square for William Penn, many different governmental bodies and many different designers have contributed to the open green spaces in the historic area around Independence Hall; but credit for recent achievements goes primarily to Edmund N. Bacon, executive director of the Philadelphia City Planning Commission.

In 1947, shortly after the *Architectural Review* of London suggested a similar plan for the bombed area around St. Paul's, Bacon proposed that the redevelopment of the blighted neighborhood southeast of Independence Hall spare all salvageable old buildings, and that the most important historic structures be connected by a continuous system of parks and footpaths, many cutting through existing blocks. With their intimate scale, constantly changing views, and picturesque juxtapositions of old and new, such greenways as have been built seem more lively, and kinder to the prevalent eighteenth- and early nineteenth-century architecture than the Mall, too grand for the domestic scale of Independence Hall, or the National Historical Park, where fine old buildings, robbed of their neighbors, stand in an isolation rarely intended by their designers.

1. Franklin Square, 1683
2. Washington Square, 1683
3. Independence Hall, 1732–41
4. Independence Mall, 1950–69
5. "Third Block of the Mall," 1963
6. Independence National Historical Park, 1960
7. Apartment towers, 1964
8. Pedestrian greenway, 1975
9. Delancey Street sitting area, 1961

Dan Kiley, landscape architect; Harbeson Hough Livingston & Larson, architects: Third Block of Independence Mall (No. 5 on plan), Philadelphia, 1963.

Covering an entire city block at the far end of the Mall and confined by a low sitting-wall, a raised brick platform has been tightly organized in a twice-repeated geometric pattern of radiating fountains that recalls the five original squares of Penn's Philadelphia. Incorporated into the design are geometric forests of honey locusts, and rows of magnolias set into rectangular planting beds. Benches too are part of the pattern. There is little incentive to move about, as the floor level is constant and any twelfth of the park tells the entire story.

The three central fountains are splendid. Great jets leap into the air, splatter down upon a four-part convex slab of granite, then slide off into a square shallow basin lined with black glass mosaic.

Wilhelm V. von Moltke, Philadelphia City Planning Commission: Delancey Street sitting area (No. 9 on plan), Philadelphia, 1961.

The pedestrian greenway opens up new views as it twists and turns through the city blocks. Occasionally, as here, it widens to become a tiny neighborhood park.

parks and plazas

Holger Blom, Stockholm Park Department: Berzelii Park, Stockholm.

An exuberantly planted pond serves as moat to separate the public park (on far bank) from the garden restaurant of an hotel, but music from the restaurant wafts free over the water to the park's café.

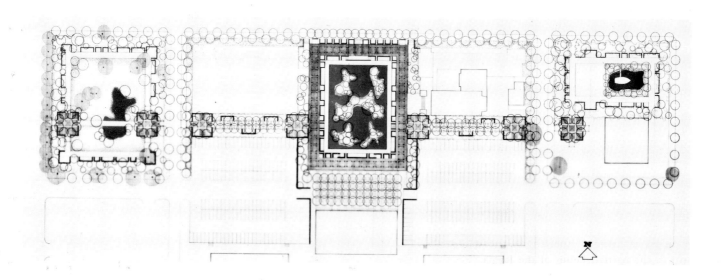

Isamu Noguchi and Louis I. Kahn: Proposed Adele Levy Memorial Playground, Riverside Drive, New York, 1964.

No conventional playground, this is a world a child can make of what he will, fancy free. His adventure would be based on stimulating materials: great grass-sheathed mounds enlivened by water chutes; shallow streams and pools; flights of steps for climbing, some forming a pyramid, others (front left) coming together as an informal amphitheater. Set into and under the grass hillside are indoor playrooms (rear left).

Noguchi first proposed an earth-sculptured playground in 1933. This latest scheme, if realized, will be a joyous release for children and a major work of civic art.

LEFT. Ian McHarg: Project for Town Center Park, South West Washington, D.C., 1962.

For a newly redeveloped area of Washington that desperately needed intelligible open space, McHarg proposed this urbane park. The spine of the project is a formal tree-lined walkway, enlivened by sitting-niches and square outdoor rooms, which leads from a playground at the east to a central water garden, surrounded and contained by a loggia, then on to a romantic landscape garden at the west. Parking space is provided at the south.

The focal water garden develops Oriental themes. Strongly contoured islands, planted with evergreens, would appear in changing perspective as one walked about the basin in the partial shelter of the loggia.

parks and plazas

Zion & Breen: Grounds of the International Hotel, John F. Kennedy International Airport, New York, 1961.

Clumps of Lombardy poplar, planted in identical gravel circles, protect the hotel from sight and sound of the airport highway. These are far more formal than Capability Brown's famous clumps, but in both cases the rhythmic arrangement of groups of trees gives a feeling of openness, and of liveliness in depth.

Zion & Breen: Grounds of the American National Exhibition, Moscow, 1959.

The landscape architects worked with refreshing modesty to encourage free circulation from one part of the exhibition to another, through an existing stand of larch trees in Moscow's Sokolniki Park.

Compacted earth covered with a thin layer of yellow sand provided a walking surface within which free-form grass islands were used to organize the trees into rhythmic groups.

LEFT. Skidmore, Owings & Merrill, with Hertzka & Knowles, associated architects: Crown Zellerbach Plaza, San Francisco, 1959.

Smooth limestone walks are set into a swirling pavement of black pebbles, and granite retaining walls loom above banks planted with ivy and wild strawberry. The shallow limestone steps have broad irregular treads, useful also as seats.

An overall view of this sunken plaza is shown on page 44.

parks and plazas

the view from above

In Ohio and Wisconsin are prehistoric mounds so vast that the symbolic shape of eagle, snake, or panther can be deciphered only from an airplane. Our own artists may one day mold and carve for the air view. Meanwhile we take pleasure in the sculpture of the natural landscape and find that distance sometimes lends enchantment even to intrinsically dreary man-scapes.

More than any people before us we take the down-view, and as we look out from our tall buildings gardens become pure pattern, as remote and insubstantial as pebbles glinting in a deep clear pool.

Thirty or so years ago the builders of Rockefeller Center set aside some of their legally buildable land as permanent public open space that would contribute not only to the amenity of their own tall buildings, but to the pleasure of everyone in the vicinity. The most distinguished of today's urban office-towers follow this precedent, occasionally with a far more generous ratio of open space to built-over land. Common denominators of the new plazas are elaborate waterworks and a strong composition that can be read from offices high above. Otherwise they differ remarkably in the way they are related to proprietary skyscrapers and to the public streets. Some are little more than a broadening of the sidewalk to include fountains and planting beds. Others are set above or below the level of the street to gain relief from distracting traffic and to give the visitor a sense of arrival. Some, with a formality mitigated only by feathery treetops and elusive *jets d'eau*, extend to the outdoors the architecture of the parent building. Others are oases of freedom within the geometry of the city.

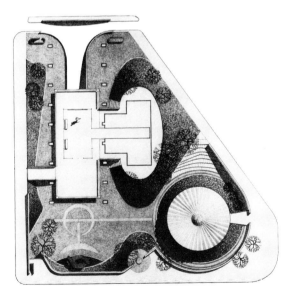

Skidmore, Owings & Merrill, with Hertzka & Knowles, associated architects: Crown Zellerbach Building and Plaza, San Francisco, 1959.

The forms of this very generous plaza are "free," yet purposefully and precisely shaped to bring together the disparate geometry of a sloping triangular site, a squat circular bank building (lower right), and the high rectangular prism of the twenty-story building, San Francisco's first glass-walled office tower.

Set into the hill and sunk as much as thirteen feet below bordering streets, the plaza is seen primarily from above. Easy access and possible seating are limited to the fan of delightfully irregular stone steps visible just above the fluted roof of the bank. As the view on page 42 suggests, those who make the descent are rewarded by textured, patterned paving, subtly mounded, variously planted earth banks, and a pool (at lower left, between countered arcs of earth and pavement) splattered by the intricate play of a winged bronze fountain.

Eywin Langkilde: Courtyard of the Baltica Insurance Company, Copenhagen.

Designed for spectators in a tall office building as well as for pedestrian pleasures, the court starts as a composition of interlocked rectangles of grass, water, and granite paving, then seems deliberately thrown off by lopped corners, skewed sculpture, and irregularities of the pool coping.

LEFT. Sven Hansen: Gardens of a hospital near Copenhagen.

The gardens are boldly drawn for view from the hospital that rises high above. The main promenade steps across a rectangular pool and curves down through a fan of stepped terraces. Like the pool, the terraces are strangely elongated and empty—an effect accentuated by the elaboration of detail at their far ends, where benches face low plants and tiny runnels. Then the walkway enters a parterre of lawn (far left) set with bright square flower boxes and granite paving blocks. Shapes again seem intentionally dislocated.

C. Th. Sørensen: Church Plaza, Kalundborg, Denmark, 1952.

Low mottled hedges make diagonals of interlocking squares, separated by zigzag grass paths. The extraordinary formality was perhaps evoked by the importance of the old church that overshadows the plaza.

The landscape architect is also, surprisingly, inventor of that least formal kind of urban play place, the *skrammellegeplads* ("junk playground," "adventure playground," or "Robinson Crusoe playground"), which he proposed in 1931 and first executed in 1941 in Copenhagen.

the view from above

Roberto Burle Marx: Roof garden and parterre, Ministry of Education, Rio de Janeiro, Brazil, 1945.

The famous Ministry was designed by a group of Brazilian architects, with Le Corbusier as consultant. The main building is a fourteen-story slab raised high on columns. Under it and at a right angle is this low wing, roofed with a garden accessible from the Minister's suite and visible from the offices above. The free forms and massed native plants of the roof garden are repeated in ground-level planting.

"The Minister's garden, seen from above," wrote Burle Marx, "is as defined as an abstract painting on my drawing board; yet when you actually walk in it, the raised foliage beds and the groups of bird-of-paradise flowers are volumes in movement."

Roberto Burle Marx: Garden of the Hospital da Lagoa, Rio de Janeiro, Brazil, 1957.

As one looks down from the tall hospital building, garden and outdoor sitting room become an abstraction. Elements are sharply differentiated, and interdependent in relationships fraught with strong unresolved tensions.

Foil to the arc of blue-tiled wall is the blood-red foliage of massed *Iresine herbstii* Hook., a tropical/temperate member of the amaranth family.

Isamu Noguchi, designer; Skidmore, Owings & Merrill, architects: Sunken court in the plaza of the Chase Manhattan Bank Building, New York, 1964.

The plaza is set over a basement extension of the bank's skyscraper, a few feet above the turbulent streets of Lower Manhattan. A hole punched into its terrazzo pavement lights basement corridors and makes a sunken court. Here Noguchi has shaped a mountain-water landscape. Hollowed as though by erosion and paved in circles broken by long wavy grooves, the granite floor recalls the raked sand of Ryōanji (page 12) in that it suggests water even when water is absent. Set into the mounds are choice rocks from Japan.

Luis Barragán: Garden originally owned by the architect, Pedregal Gardens, Mexico, D.F., 1951.

The encroachment of lava and wild vegetation upon concrete podium and white-painted iron fence suggests complex, ambivalent relationships between man and nature. Artifact and natural fact are separate, antagonistic, yet made mutually dependent by the tensions between them.

gardens and flower gardens

A shared characteristic of modern gardens is openness to view and access from adjacent buildings, provided that those buildings too are "modern" in design; and when walls are glass an adjoining garden must be convincing even when deciduous trees have lost their leaves and herbaceous plants have bowed to frost. Otherwise they differ remarkably. Some offer the ancient pleasures of digging, planting, smelling, sitting, strolling. Some provide for playing, swimming, all manner of activity. Others serve mainly for the enjoyment of sculpture or water, or for a view from above. Beyond such functional differences is the question, often debatable, as to whether nature is used for an experience of art, or art for an experience of nature.

Flowers as such are not indispensable to a garden, and formal beds are today generally restricted, as in China, to courtyards or terraces of buildings. The idea of a garden as above all a place to grow flowers is something of a nineteenth-century invention: fascinated by horticulture, the Victorians crowded their lawns with showy exotics bedded out in whimsical patterns. Reaction started in the 1860s when William Robinson urged the use of hardy plants that would harmonize with the English landscape, and showed how flowers could be naturalized in meadow and woodland. Gertrude Jekyll pursued similar ideas, but with a new feeling for eloquent relationships of forms, colors, and textures, evident both in her famous borders and in her less formal planting. If we now think of a garden as continuous in space rather than as Miss Jekyll's isolated "living pictures," her contribution is still impressive.

The day of the red geranium is not over. Turning up, fashionably, in the most alien circumstances, it is presumably treasured for the shock of unrelatedness as well as the shock of color. Many sensitive designers, however, are wary of obvious exotics. They prefer native plants, or such imported plants as have a natural affinity with the site and with each other. Interested in structure and foliage, they may reveal extraordinary beauty in ordinary weeds and field grasses. They avoid heterogeneous assortments, and often dramatize the differences between plants by playing one kind and color of massed vegetation against another.

If the dynamic interplay of massed plants quickly identifies a garden as belonging to our own day, it is only one approach. Since Burle Marx has dealt most variously with massed plants, it must be noted that this Brazilian plantsman, master of swirling carpets and geometric patchwork, now sometimes chooses to explore interrelationships of plants and land (page 63) of an order more subtle than could be suggested by any formal counterplay of masses. And Barragán's idea of a garden is something different again.

ABOVE. Lawrence Halprin: Roof garden, San Francisco, 1952.

A contrapuntal relationship has been established between the formal modular framework, implied even when omitted, and the rhythmic disposition of plants and rocks. The selection of rocks and gravel shows a fine sense of local scale.

Gabriel Guevrékian: Garden for the Comte de Noailles, Hyères, France, 1925.

The square concrete frames are identical in size. Some are filled with massed tulips, others set flush with colored tile. Unusual in more recent gardens of this kind is the central axis, focusing attention on the sculpture by Lipchitz.

ABOVE. Roberto Burle Marx: Terrace for Inocente Palacios, overlooking Caracas, Venezuela, 1957.

Two kinds of grass checker the terrace with squares of light green and dark in a pattern related to the pavement of the platform. Other vegetation takes its own bold forms.

Alexander Girard: Patio of his own house, Santa Fé, New Mexico, 1954.

A famous exhibition designer, Girard drew his materials from New Mexico's living desert and juxtaposed them to dramatize their unique qualities. Set below a loggia, the modular composition is seen primarily from above.

gardens and flower gardens

Dan Kiley, landscape architect; Skidmore, Owings & Merrill, architects: Air Garden, U.S. Air Force Academy, Colorado Springs, Colorado, 1959.

The water garden is seven hundred feet long, running from the cadet dormitories to the dining hall shown below. It lies in a part of the Academy that is open to the public only on pre-arranged tours.

Since the eastern slopes of the Rocky Mountains are very dry, but cool, this oasis offers pools, fountains, and full sunlight. Yet water plays a secondary role, for the dominant horizontal plane is not the surface of the water, but the level of the walkways that skirt and bridge the lowered pools. Greenery is limited to evergreen hedges and a surrounding grove of regularly spaced honey locusts.

There is more than a touch of the Grand Manner in the vastness, the axial symmetry, and the military precision of the garden, but the offset walks are obviously designed for strolling rather than parade.

Edwin Lutyens: Mughal Gardens (originally the gardens of the Viceroy's Palace), New Delhi, India, 1911–31.

With its crossed canals, symbolic of the four rivers of Paradise, a Moslem's garden has been his heaven on earth.

In these national pleasure gardens—brilliant foil to bright silk saris and still the favorite stage for large official parties—the British architect gave new life to the Moslem tradition of northern India. Working between the levels of the brimful canals and the broad bridges, a grade difference of less than two feet, he developed a three-dimensional geometric composition of remarkable richness, remarkable simplicity. Water dominates, everywhere, but trees and hedges are more important now than in this early photograph.

gardens and flower gardens

Herbert Bayer: The Grass Mound, Aspen Meadows Hotel, Aspen, Colorado, 1955.

Sunk within an earth bank forty feet in diameter are a circular mound, a circular hole, and a rough granite boulder. From the inside the bank rises above eye-level to give a sense of enclosure.

The sculptured outdoor room is set easily into a billowy meadow planted with little groves of quaking aspen and threaded by the narrow man-made stream visible in the foreground. At another end of the meadow is the marble garden shown on page 36.

Ernst Cramer: "Poet's Garden" at the 1959 Garden Exhibition, Zurich, Switzerland.

Triangular earth mounds and a stepped cone were precisely edged, grass-sheathed, and doubled by a still pool.

The garden was not so much a garden as sculpture to walk through—abstract earth shapes independent of place, with sharp arrises foreign to the nature of their material.

Paolo Soleri: Cosanti Foundation, Scottsdale, Arizona, begun 1962.

Earth excavated from the desert floor for sunken courts and vaulted pavilions was carved into inclined planes, one of which serves as footpath from the entrance courtyard.

The suburban lot was originally level and characterless. Soleri's partially submerged architecture, turning in on itself in unexpected ways, makes a world apart, and its low profile is a neighborly civility.

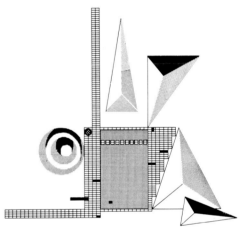

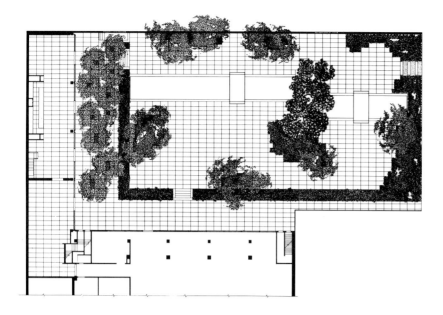

Philip Johnson, architect; James Fanning, landscape architect: The Abby Aldrich Rockefeller Sculpture Garden, The Museum of Modern Art, New York, 1953.

The garden is distinguished by a lively, mutually respectful relationship among architecture, sculpture, and plants, and by a fine reciprocity between formality and freedom. Architectural elements, including pools, are geometric. Planting is not geometric. Trees are neither clipped nor mathematically spaced, but generally clustered in groups of a single species—cryptomeria, birch, European hornbeam, or weeping beech—to serve as space division and sculpture background, or as leafy canopy. Others are decorative silhouettes against gray brick walls.

Rectangular paving slabs of gray marble unify the two ground planes even as they encourage free circulation. Inset planting beds are rectilinear, but free of rigidity. Low planting is massed, with each bed or bank limited to a single kind of permanent ground cover or transitory flower.

The garden illustrated here is changed and expanded by 1964 and 1984 additions to the Museum, including two new wings and a glass-walled escalator hall.

gardens and flower gardens

Pietro Porcinai, landscape architect; Belgiojoso, Peressutti & Rogers, architects: Private park, Saronno, Italy.

In the Lombardy plain Porcinai has fashioned a private world, walled from its surroundings. The water garden illustrated above is near the entrance, but the gentle rise of an artificial hill protects it from street noise even as it hides the confining wall and the porter's lodge. There is something indigenously Italian in the scale and splendor and sobriety of this concocted landscape, yet no trace of nostalgia for the Italian Renaissance is evident in the rhythmic composition.

Private park, Saronno.

Flowers are concentrated in the *viale fiorito* (left), the flower-carpeted avenue that bisects the park. Unexpectedly, there is no terminal focus. The long jagged mat of massed annuals, changed with the seasons, is its own reason for existence. Unexpected, again, is the placing of sculpture off-center in the grassy verge.

Roberto Burle Marx: Carlos Somlo garden, Persepolis, Brazil, 1948.

Characteristic of the fine art of Burle Marx has been the massing of indigenous plants as a splendid swirling interplay of textured colors that violates neither the integrity of the individual plant nor the integrity of the large landscape.

The effect is achieved through foliage rather than flowers, and even the lawn, like a beach at ebb tide, is patterned in waves of green, gray, and yellowish grass.

Roberto Burle Marx: Delfino garden, Caracas, Venezuela, 1960.

Boulders are set into a hummocky hill sheathed with soft Japanese *zoysia* and crowned with feathery grass. At the left are water plants, a miniature pond, and a view back into the dense shade of a mango grove.

Here is no obvious patterning through contrasts of massed plants, and none of the "free" forms that—unless developed in close relation to ground contours—can look as arbitrarily imposed as the forms of geometry. Far less formal than the artist's best known gardens of the past, and spatially more developed, this small constructed landscape has the kind of freedom, inner order, and inevitability that we associate with wildness, yet rarely find so articulately presented in wild nature.

gardens and flower gardens

Eero Saarinen & Associates, architects; Sasaki, Walker & Associates, landscape architects: IBM Research Center, Yorktown Heights, New York, 1960.

A segment of a circle, the thousand-foot-long building hugs the contours of a crescent hill and surveys a sweep of country through its glass front.

The rear of the building, shown here, curves around a court dug well back into the slope. Spanning this dry moat are footbridges leading to employees' parking lots further up the hill. The garden, normally seen from above, has no fashionable boulders, no fussy details—only green islands washed by a sea of white gravel and a low yew hedge to screen ducts and service stairs. The grassy islands, mounded for plastic interest, are a quiet background for willow and crabapple trees.

LEFT. Ralph Stevens: Succulent garden for Warren Tremaine, Santa Barbara, California, 1949.

High jagged heads of giant yucca and aloe are recalled in great earthborne bursts of agave that bring the eye down to smaller massed succulents of myriad shapes and colors. The landscape architect brought plants from many places to form a natural community—and a community that seems natural to this particular sunny slope. Even the hillocks of Korean grass (Japanese *zoysia*) that soften the transition from domestic terrace to inhospitable spiky succulents support the feeling of ecological validity. Yet there is no literal imitation of nature: the juxtaposition of colors and forms has the freedom and eloquence of an abstract painting. Working independently of Burle Marx, Stevens arrived at some similar conclusions.

Adjoining a house designed for the Tremaines by Richard Neutra, the Stevens garden seems to be what Neutra called for when he wrote in 1936 that a garden should be "an ensemble of plants that can keep natural company."

Luis Barragán: Private garden, Mexico, D.F., 1942.

Even in this early garden, designed by Barragán for himself and later sold, there is an emphatic use of walls—not free-standing walls as later at Pedregal Gardens and Las Arboledas, but massive stone retaining walls. Three such walls define a rectangular pool (right middle ground) and ascending terraces.

The wall of the middle terrace becomes a stairway as it steps up to the top of the garden. There are no railings, but potted plants suggest safety.

gardens and flower gardens

gardens in a natural landscape

More than a building, a garden is difficult to insert into a broad natural landscape. If it is not to intrude, its design must be consonant with the natural rhythms of the site and the character of the native vegetation. Burle Marx has shown that planting need not be naturalistic to play an harmonious role in open country; but this takes great skill.

Exclusion of imported plants would be affectation. What seems more indigenous to California and Mexico than Australian eucalyptus? Yet the greatest designers like to work with plant communities that are native to the site—in appearance if not always in fact.

A garden can belong, and not just to its immediate place, for we know better than our ancestors that a given site is only part of the whole, and this too can find expression, even when coherence and continuity and freedom seem difficult to reconcile with privacy, perhaps also with the desire to create a self-sufficient work of art. As a Sung landscape painter observed, design can go out at the sides to suggest the infinity of nature.

In the hands of a true landscape artist the inherent quality of a place is not ignored, but may be so intensified that man feels here, *here* in touch with its very essence. Through art he is placed in communication with its genius.

LEFT AND ABOVE. Roberto Burle Marx: Garden for Odete Monteiro, Corrêas, near Petrópolis, Brazil, 1947.

Shapes of boulders, low plants, and mountains are to a large extent analogous. Other plants are strong receding verticals that point to the mountains even as their changing perspectives bring the distant view actively into the garden. Plant materials are indigenous, and the garden's biomorphic plan (above) seems inspired by the natural contours of the site.

Roberto Burle Marx: Garden for Alberto Kronsforth, Teresópolis, Brazil, 1956.

Formal and boldly artificial as it is, the curvilinear carpet-bedding seems less an intrusion than an elaboration of themes implicit in the natural landscape.

Philip Johnson: Grounds of the architect's own house, New Canaan, Connecticut. Jet built in 1961, pavilion in 1963.

Seen from the glass-walled house, perched on a terrace sixty feet above the artificial pond, water leaps one-hundred-and-twenty feet into the air to unify meadows, woods, hills, and sky. Night illumination is discreetly limited to silver and gold, simulating moonlight and daylight, and the pump is effectively muffled.

The addition of the water pavilion, built at two-thirds normal scale, creates strong new tensions in the landscape. The pavilion extends pinwheel arms even as it shrinks back into geometric self-sufficiency, and its diminutive size makes the great jet (unfortunately not photographed at full height) more overpowering than ever.

Thomas D. Church: Garden and pool for Dewey Donnell, Sonoma, California, 1948. Sculptured island by Adaline Kent.

Related neither to buildings nor to land form, most swimming pools are literally for swimmers only. This pool is an exception. Its fluid shaping was inspired by the winding creeks of salt marshes seen through the frame of live oaks. The large landscape is expanded, not denied.

gardens in a natural landscape

Luis Barragán: Private gardens in the subdivision of Pedregal Gardens, Mexico, D.F., 1949–51.

If the land had been developed according to Barragán's conception, response to the unique splendor of the volcanic site would have been brilliant. He specified large lots with high peripheral walls built of the rough local lava rock, in its own purplish black or occasionally stained with color, and opened up here and there by fences of tall iron pickets (page 50). Rising and falling with the land, and affirming rather than denying its character and continuity, the majestic walls were to enclose houses of quiet but unequivocally modern design and gardens that would respect both the existing lava formations and the extraordinary natural vegetation. There was to be no gentling, no formalizing, no petty prettifying.

Illustrated at left and right are model gardens in which he incorporated some of his ideas. Steps are carved into the living rock and the level lawn looks as though it had been poured between the congealed waves of lava. Walls of the same dark stone are so disposed that the somber mountains seem drawn into the garden. The fantastic beauty of native plants and rocks is somehow made more accessible by the hand of man.

The garden shown below is different. Here art intensifies nature less by entering and changing it than by separating itself in a strange reciprocal relationship. The push of writhing wilderness into the neat rectangular pool seems ominous.

ABOVE AND RIGHT. Jens Jensen: Columbus Park, Chicago, 1918.

Jensen was working within the great landscape tradition when early in this century he brought to metropolitan Chicago the essence of the Illinois prairies as he understood them.

"Take native plants," he said, "and let them govern each other." This was understatement. A fine sense of ecological fitness was indeed the basis for his work at Columbus Park, but it was with a highly developed feeling for formal and spatial relationships that he laid out meadows and waters, planted forests of maple and oak, elm and ash, and emphasized the low horizontals of his vision with masses of wild roses and native shrubs. The park was as deliberately composed as Noguchi's marble "landscape."

constructed landscapes

In the eighteenth century land preserved its basic integrity: town was town, country was country, and wilderness needed no Congressional guaranty. Now the land has been so ironed out by urban sprawl, so grayed down, that its genius will often be sought in vain.

The artist in this case starts with a more or less clean slate. He may use the opportunity to concoct a wholly artificial composition, a lunar landscape disconnected from its particular place on earth. Or he may choose to set limits to his own freedom. Preserving and enhancing any possibly positive values of the site, and keeping in mind the characteristic land forms of the region as well as its native flora, he may compose a landscape that will seem at once free and inevitable.

In a manner of speaking, every work of landscape art is a fresh construction. Even if the designer does nothing more than add or subtract a single tree, he re-creates the scene by his will to form.

Isamu Noguchi, sculptor; Skidmore, Owings & Merrill, architects: Sunken court in the plaza of the Beinecke Rare Book Library, Yale University, New Haven, Connecticut, 1963.

Noguchi has carved an "imaginary landscape" of white marble. On the grooved platform are three symbolic shapes—a pyramid (matter), a hollow disc (the sun, or energy), and a poised cube (chance, or the condition of man).

73

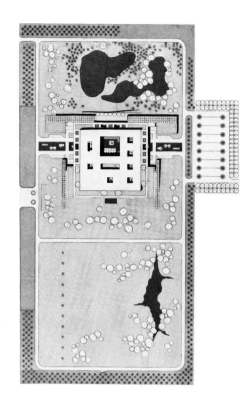

Skidmore, Owings & Merrill, architects; Sasaki, Walker & Associates, landscape consultants: The Upjohn Company, Kalamazoo, Michigan, 1961.

The architects have developed their own way of dealing with the large office building that is set in spacious country. In this characteristic example the building—complete with formal terraces and courtyards (see page 20)—is raised above the idealized landscape on a broad fieldstone podium. Rectangular basins reach out to parking lots at either side, but the line of demarcation between geometric and non-geometric is otherwise firmly drawn.

Within the formal quincunx planting of pines that protects the eighty-acre site, the landscape architects have constructed a scene inspired by Michigan's lake-dotted countryside. Willows were planted along the man-made lagoons, birches on middle ground, pines and sugar maples above.

Skidmore, Owings & Merrill: Connecticut General Life Insurance Company, Bloomfield, Connecticut, 1957.

Office building and formal terrace are again decisively separated from gently naturalized surroundings.

The view from the building (below) was carefully composed in the landscape style. An eighteenth-century Englishman might be puzzled by Noguchi's "Family Group" in red sandstone, but he would understand the broad sweep of meadow down to the serpentine pond, the disposition of trees, and the rise to the focal sculpture, silhouetted against dense woods.

constructed landscapes

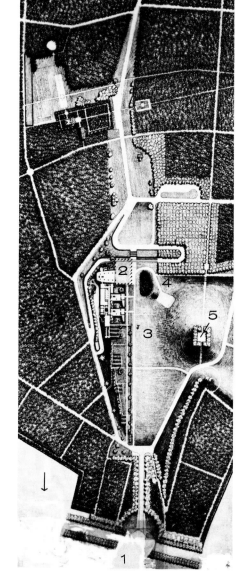

1. Entrance
2. Crematorium
3. Cross
4. Pond and
ceremonial site
5. Meditation place

Gunnar Asplund and Sigurd Lewerentz: Forest Cemetery (Skogskyrko-gården), Stockholm. Commissioned as result of a 1914 international competition. Executed 1917–40. Crematorium and ceremonial site designed by Asplund and built 1937–40. (See also pages 78–79.)

Confronting cross and sky, mourners walk the long upward path to the crematorium, then follow the ashes to their burial place in the pine forests. Experience of earth and sky is intense.

This is a created landscape, for the northern part of the tract came to hand as a nondescript pine-covered slope hollowed by gravel pits. Now it is transformed into a world apart and one moves within a vast earth sculpture, shaped by great grassy mounds that screen off the sight and sound of adjacent highway and rapid transit line. Motor traffic is removed from the main approach, which is reserved for the pedestrian.

constructed landscapes

Forest Cemetery, Stockholm (continued).

The atrium of the crematorium looks across a man-made pond to the paved apron which Asplund conceived as a site for great public funeral services. Crowning the rise are the low walls of a meditation place, with sparse delicate trees silhouetted against the enormous sky and the vast rolling surface of the earth.

From the cemetery entrance one sees that steps, carved into the slope of the further mound, mount to the retreat at its summit.

constructed landscapes

In pre-industrial societies man is so close to the land that he seems unable to do it visible wrong. Villages and towns appear to grow out of the ground, and temples seem dedicated to the *genius loci* as well as to the gods above. All this has changed. Even farming has become an industry and a business. Now the old feeling for the land is recaptured only occasionally, by design, and rarely at a scale larger than that of an individual building and its parcel of ground.

One school of thought insists that architecture, the pure creation of man's spirit, be wholly independent of its natural setting, to which it then serves as complement and foil. Although, as ex-Dean Hudnut of Harvard observed, a meadow with a house in it is not quite the same as a meadow without a house, yet the integrity of a landscape is at least theoretically preserved when buildings stand aloof, self-contained, respectfully alien, and when neither gardens nor terraces mediate between what is strictly architectural and what is natural or naturalized. Implied in the contrast is a relationship of a kind—the dynamic relationship of opposites. The concept goes back, of course, to eighteenth-century England (page 9), where rough-cropped meadows lapped the elegant walls of Palladian great houses, but it was given new life and form in our own century by Le Corbusier, particularly in those famous buildings that hover free of the ground on stilts, with fields and ponds brought up to the supports, even washing beyond them, and all provision for outdoor living relegated to the roofs.

Other architects prefer to modify the pure landscape style. Evidently agreeing with Humphrey Repton (d. 1818) that "the gardens or pleasure grounds near a house may be considered as so many apartments belonging to its state, its comfort, and its pleasure," they arrange indoor and outdoor living space together as a geometric entity, raised upon a low platform and set upon a countryside otherwise disturbed as little as possible.

A third approach makes no fast distinction between the artifact and the facts of nature. Buildings are not strangers to the land, for everything is done to give a sense of interpenetration between architecture and its natural surroundings. This is the kind of design originally associated with Frank Lloyd Wright, whose firm stipulation was that a building finally appear to belong to its site—of it, not on it; and it was his sensitive response to the individuality of a site that made him superbly a landscape artist.

A spiralling urban population makes the large problems of land use infinitely complex, but if we are to move toward a total environment that will affirm life in rich diversity, patterns of living and building must again be brought into harmony with the land; and since each place on earth is unique, we must trust the beguiling abstractions of master plans only when they conserve and intensify the elusive realities of their very particular sites.

Frank Lloyd Wright: Taliesin West, the architect's winter camp near Scottsdale, Arizona. Begun 1937.

Sloping walls were molded of coarse concrete and great desert rocks—rose, gold, rust, green, gray, orange-rimmed, quartz-streaked, and black-speckled. Above went a slanted roof of redwood and canvas.

With its formal triangular terrace, jutting out into the wilderness like the prow of a ship, Taliesin West is a "platform house" penetrated by the desert. Woven into its fabric are rocks, cactus, mountain, light. Its space is the space of the desert, made accessible to man through art.

Luis Barragán: Street intersection, Las Arboledas, State of Mexico, 1958–62.

The long stucco wall runs over the horizon to affirm the continuity of the land. Foil to the upswept wall is the tilted plane of the traffic island.

Le Corbusier: Apartment house at Nantes-Rezé, France, 1955.

Precisely defined as a closed volume and lifted from the ground on stilts, the building is as independent of its surroundings as it could well be. No terraces, no gardens. Architecture and landscape preserve their separate identities, and outdoor living is relegated to the rooftop as at Marseilles (page 23).

buildings and the land

Eliot Noyes: House of the architect, New Canaan, Connecticut, 1955.

    The garden may be set within the building—in archetypal manner—to make a human enclave in the howling wilderness.

Edward L. Barnes: Henry Kaufmann Campgrounds, Wyandanch, New York, 1962.

    Eye-shaped swimming pools and concrete walks follow the contours of the slope at three different levels. Their fluid lines are broken and invigorated by the sudden—and logical—right angles of the cross-contour steps that connect them.

Edward L. Barnes: Robert Osborn house, Salisbury, Connecticut, 1951.

Indoor and outdoor living space form a geometric entity, an island in the flowery fields. In the architect's words, "The contrast between untouched nature and the area for living is dramatized in the platform plan. The garden is conceived as part of the house. Its wall is an extension of the house foundation; enclosed terraces complement inside spaces. Shade trees make a leafy outdoor ceiling."

buildings and the land

83

Serge Chermayeff, architect; Christopher Tunnard, landscape consultant: Chermayeff house, near Halland, Sussex, England, 1937.

Set with its living-gardens on a low brick platform at the edge of the woods, the house maintains its separate identity, yet extends long arms to embrace the gentle Sussex countryside.

The beech forest was carefully thinned as it met the meadow, and thousands of daffodils were scattered beneath the trees. At the glass-sheltered end of the projecting terrace, splendid against the idyllic background, was a large reclining figure by Henry Moore.

Looking back on his work, Chermayeff said that "shaping the place" was more important than the house itself.

Alvar Aalto: Maison Carré, Bazoches, near Paris, 1961.

Broad, loosely planted steps, set easily into the contours, modulate the passage from geometry to nature, and anchor the house firmly to the ground.

buildings and the land

New York State Department of Public Works: Upper reaches of the Taconic State Parkway, New York, 1933–63.

Northbound and southbound roadways are independent, each free to pursue its future along the natural contours most favorable to it. There is a minimum of cut and fill, of new planting, of tampering of any kind. Woods and fields and rock outcrops are penetrated by concrete ribbons that are less an interruption of the landscape than an affirmation of its topography.

Luis Barragán: Main boulevard, Pedregal Gardens, Mexico, D.F., 1949.

Highway and landscape encroach upon each other, yet maintain separate integrities. Their relationship is as violent as the volcanic wasteland itself—a sea of lava with petrified waves.

Charles Eames: Eames house, Pacific Palisades, California, 1949.

Composed of two austere boxes, the house defers to the landscape only in its imaginative placement.

Rather than destroy the beautiful natural meadow high over the ocean, Eames pushed his house far back into the steep hillside, behind the shelter of giant eucalyptus trees. The excavated earth he used to make a protective mound on the one adjacent property line.

Planted with rye grass—yellow in the dry season—and with a scattering of wild flowers, the meadow has reverted to nature, and the house seems alone in the world with its wild windblown garden and the sea.

buildings and the land

ABOVE. Frank Lloyd Wright, Aaron G. Green, and The Taliesin Associates: Marin County Civic Center, San Rafael, California.

When finally completed according to the plans of 1958, the building will double its present length, and the tiered arches of the new block will die away against the slopes of a large freestanding mound far off to the left, out of the picture.

Wright's usual practice was to run his buildings parallel with the natural contours. Here he has built across the contours, yet without loss of harmony between architecture and landscape. Contributing to the rightness of the building in its setting is the analogy between the low segmental arches, the flattened dome, and the gentle earth mounds peculiar to the region.

Burnham Hoyt: Red Rocks Amphitheater for Denver, Morrison, Colorado, 1941.

Fitted into the slope of the eastern foothills of the Rockies as they rise abruptly from the Colorado plateau, the music theater lies between huge natural outcrops of upthrusting red sandstone. Each seat looks over the stage to a shimmer of plains melting into the far flat horizon, at night to the distant twinkle of city lights.

Alden B. Dow: House and garden of the architect, Midland, Michigan, 1941.

Architecture, water, and native plants are interwoven with an art that is ultimately self-effacing. The indivisibility of house and setting is affirmed by the rhythmic descent of gently sloped roofs, to end over a living room sunk into the pond—affirmed again by the concrete building blocks that step out into the water as though finally freed of rational constraints.

Frank Lloyd Wright: Taliesin, the architect's own house at Spring Green, Wisconsin. 1911, 1914, 1925.

The transition from house and studio to courtyards, gardens and farm buildings, and on to meadows and orchards, fields and woodland, is scarcely perceptible, so subtly is one part related to another and all to the contours and character of the land.

"I knew well," Wright wrote in his autobiography, "that no house should ever be *on* a hill or *on* anything. It should be *of* the hill. Belonging to it. Hill and house should live together each the happier for the other."

buildings and the land

Oscar Niemeyer: House for the architect, Rio de Janeiro, 1954.

Perforated by a pool and punctuated by a monstrous boulder, the sculptured terrace elaborates the bold irregular curves of the roof slab that overshadows it. Niemeyer's retreat is a powerfully assertive, yet harmonious new force among the bold irregular curves of the wild landscape.

Frank Lloyd Wright: Fallingwater, house for Edgar J. Kaufmann, Sr., Bear Run, near Mill Run, Pennsylvania, 1937. (Given to the Western Pennsylvania Conservancy in 1963, Fallingwater is now open to the public.)

The house is set boldly into the wild with no terrace or garden as passage of transition, yet with an empathy between structure and landscape that is very different from the studied isolation of Le Corbusier's buildings.

Stone quarried from nearby ledges makes the massive piers. Cantilevered from them are the great reinforced-concrete slabs which carry the living space out over the water and recall, in their rhythmic stratification, the jutting ledges of the streambed.

buildings and the land

since 1964

Changes in attitude toward the natural environment have come faster than ever before, and most dramatically in the United States, where our traditional notion of endless frontiers and limitless God-given resources was quite suddenly perceived as dangerous nonsense. Even as issues of civil rights and Vietnam involvement polarized our society and alienated our young, belated recognition of galloping pollution and waste of precious resources brought us into battle on another front, this time with the very premises of our careless industrial society. As the concerns of the few became the concerns of the many, we started dreaming of a simpler kind of life that would be founded on respect for the earth and for the productivity of our own hands. Even middle-aged suburbanites scurried out to raise "organic" vegetables.

Professional attention turned to ecologically sound land-use planning at large scale, based on detailed site analysis such as the map-overlay technique devised by Ian McHarg. Not building came to seem as important as building: in 1971, year four of the *Whole Earth Catalog*, a coveted *PA* Design Citation went to a nonarchitectural scheme for lyrically unobtrusive camping on fifty-five rolling Texas acres. Preservation of natural areas became a matter of great concern, less for man's continuing enjoyment and education than for his long-term survival, which may depend upon the protection of ecological and genetic diversity from further depredation. Where valid native landscape no longer exists it has on occasion been concocted, but Darrel Morrison sees his only partial success in a diligently scientific effort to duplicate the original Wisconsin prairie as yet another warning that preservation is far preferable to attempts at reconstruction.

Everyone in the Western world who could read or hear has in these two decades been exposed to the fact that Homo sapiens is this planet's rude and possibly temporary guest, not its lord. That new general awareness, coupled with the rebellious mood of much of the period, might have been expected to provoke an esthetic revolution in landscape design—some such major change as occurred in eighteenth-century England (page 9), when a suddenly more comfortable feeling about nature produced the great "landscape style." But now we see no revolution, no widely shared agreement on a concept of design appropriate to our troubled times. Instead there are a few isolated creative spirits, here and abroad, each making his own truth, and none seeming to offer a theoretical base capable of initiating and sustaining a movement.

Berkeley, California, 1969.

War between Man and Nature? No, merely a dutiful policeman uprooting illegal plantings in the bloody People's Park skirmish of the War between Students and the Establishment, a conflict which erupted in 1964 with the Free Speech Movement of the University's highly politicized students and intensified with growing national protest against American involvement in Vietnam.

In April several hundred students and local residents had, without permission, converted a large vacant lot, owned by the University, into an instant pleasance which they named People's Park. On May 15th armed police moved in to clear the park and guard construction of a chain-link fence which would assert University ownership. The symbols seemed so clear—countercultural flowers vs. fence and weaponry—that six thousand angry people marched to the site. Stones were thrown. The response was tear gas, birdshot, buckshot, and activation of the National Guard.

On the not unreasonable assumption that a designed landscape reveals its designer's perception of the man/nature relationship, the introduction to this book identified three different mind sets: man as lord of creation, or as respectful alien, or as participant within a whole. Few designs fit neatly and completely into any one of these subjective, slippery categories, yet they can be useful in discussion.

Lord of creation is the role assumed by those few latter-day Le Nôtres who propose to impose upon land and plants the grand order of their favored architectural and urban forms, generally with heavy but "witty" reference to the classical past. To a dedicated formalist, nature presents no counter-claim and a tree is little more than a remarkably pretty, regrettably recalcitrant building material. But no important example of classicizing landscape design has apparently yet been executed, and most postmodernists handle the settings of their neo-Mannerist or neo-neoclassic or neo-Deco or neo-Vegas structures in one of the modest ways described on page 80.

Far more characteristic of today's high art than Baroque axes and topiary is a good measure of humility before the facts and forces of the natural world. The purest statement of alienation and awe may be SITE's forest-invaded non-architecture, which metaphorically concedes nature's superior strength and ultimate victory. Working out of more complex concerns, De Maria deflects the course of nearby lightning only to play up its frightful power; Halprin at Portland and Johnson at Fort Worth dramatize as never before the fearfulness of water; and even Barragán has occasionally set up disturbing confrontations, as on page 50, between geometry and vegetation.

But Barragán is basically a mystic. Like Frank Lloyd Wright, he feeds our latent sense of participation in some indefinable whole. The universe? When Charles Jencks, analyst of recent architecture, complains that Barragán suggests "cosmic meanings which are nevertheless hermetic and inaccessible to a wide audience," he overlooks the possibility that the extraordinary experience proferred by Barragán may be as available to the illiterate as to the elite, only in part because his ever more powerful color does not lend itself to facile theorizing. Whereas his post-Pedregal work affirms the flatness of the ground and seeks no change of level, the house built in Spain by his admirer, Ambasz, steps down into the earth and up into the sky in cosmic imagery so patent as perhaps to satisfy Jencks himself. Scarpa's great cemetery (page 110 and back cover) is rich in traditional, easily deciphered symbol, but its all-pervasive step motif is wonderfully ambiguous.

To quote from the 1964 preface, we share only our uncertainties. Ambiguity is the one tie that binds present-day landscape designers. The self-referential grid of repeated squares, so handsomely developed in the 1950s, is dead; and even our committed formalists wilfully pervert their projected classic symmetries. Our mood runs to the open-ended, the indeterminate, for clarity is behind us, or in front of us, but not ours at this point in time.

Walter De Maria: The Lightning Field, New Mexico, 1977.

In the late 1960s sculptors came out of their studios to attack the natural landscape at vast scale. Michael Heizer, displacer of forty thousand tons of Nevada (1969), and Robert Smithson, modeler of Great Salt Lake's fifteen-hundred-foot Spiral Jetty (1970), can be compared only to Gutzon Borglum (Four Presidents Monument, Black Hills, South Dakota, 1925–41) in the boldness with which they changed the face of nature. —*Remembered from 1940, a girl peering into the Grand Canyon—Oh my, what a lot of damage! Older woman—That's not damage, dear, that's Art.*

De Maria and Christo, rather than change the earth, complement it by opening a window into the cosmos. Too well known to require illustration are Christo's outrageous but properly temporary statements: the plastic-wrapped mile of Australian coastal cliffs (1969), the two-hundred-foot-high orange curtain slung between two Colorado peaks (1972), and in California the Running Fence of 1976.

The Lightning Field has little of Christo's extravagance. Into the wide desert valley De Maria inserted a regular grid of four hundred stainless-steel rods, spaced two hundred twenty feet apart and varied in height (averaging just under twenty-one feet) to bring their pointed tops into alignment above the rough terrain. The sight of these delicately drawn verticals, glinting under sun and moon in counterpoint to their rugged natural setting, is profoundly moving even without lightning.

SITE, architects: Forest Building, Best Products Company, 9008 Quioccasin Road, Henrico County, Richmond, Virginia, 1979–80.

As though Martians or dinosaurs were one morning found encamped in the middle of Route 1, a hopelessly ordinary commercial building is split apart by forest.

The joke, of course, is different in kind from the historicizing witticisms of postmodernism. If it is a one-liner, as some have charged, it carries an unusually heavy load of metaphor. SITE's "de-architecture" stands conventional assumptions on their heads as it shatters the finite static box with a shocking assertion of indeterminacy, change, mortality. Just as the Berkeley news photo on page 95 can be read out of context as modern man's savaging of nature, so Best's Richmond showroom suggests that violated natural systems fight back, perhaps to win.

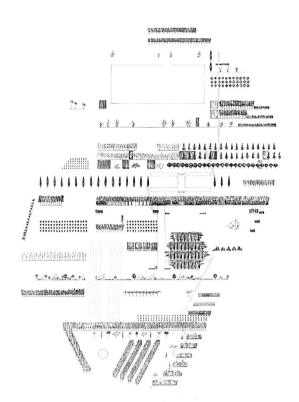

Office for Metropolitan Architecture, London branch (Rem Koolhaas): Project awarded second place in the Parc de la Villette competition, Paris, 1982–83.

Although the mission of a great city is to encourage productive interaction of diverse people and things, activities and ideas, the large urban park is traditionally a bucolic retreat. Mitterrand proposed a novel facility when he announced in 1982 a competition for the design of a park, on one hundred thirty-six desolate acres off Paris's major ring road, which would be an active generator of invention, education, and entertainment. Provision was required both for physical recreation and for multiple overlapping activities in science, technology, and the arts, primarily through thematic "discovery gardens."

The architects span the flat site with fifty-meter east-west bands, each devoted to a different program category. Long boundaries encourage interpenetration of adjacent activities, and people walking on north-south paths would have unexpected educational and recreational encounters. The planting plan (left) shows screens of trees set between the bands to suggest a depth of varying landscapes even as they provide an intelligible three-dimensional framework.

M. Paul Friedberg, landscape architect; Pomerance & Breines, architects: Riis Plaza, Jacob Riis Houses, East 6th to East 10th Streets at Avenue D, New York, 1965–66.

As customary in 1949, public-housing barracks for eight thousand people had been embellished with a grassy mall guarded from use by chain-link fencing. Funds from the Vincent Astor Foundation transformed those three acres into a jolly, lively plaza enthusiastically approved by its users. Fences and grass were replaced by a handsome series of outdoor rooms, paved to permit free circulation and shaped at varied levels as adventure playgrounds, quieter sitting areas, and a sunken multi-use amphitheater. Water plays an important role as spray, runnel, and shallow pool.

since 1964

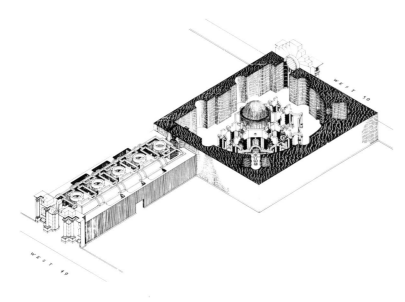

Allan Greenberg: Proposal for a park in mid-town Manhattan, New York, 1979.

Greenberg was commissioned by The Museum of Modern Art to redesign an existing mid-block public walkway consisting of a broad corridor and a square defined by an adjacent office tower and older low buildings. Recalling work by Lutyens prior to the Mughal Gardens (page 55), the architect remodelled the corridor as classical *allée*, roofed by a gilded Baroque trellis, then used an elaborately sculptured twenty-foot hedge to transform the square into a semi-circle centered by a water-domed octagonal pavilion.

Kevin Roche and John Dinkeloo, architects; Dan Kiley, landscape architect: The Ford Foundation, 320 East 43rd Street, New York, 1963–69.

First of the multi-story greenhouses which have become familiar in office buildings and hotels, this great glazed garden may still be the most attractive. Sheltered by the glass walls and roof of the building's southeast corner and overlooked by the sliding glass of twelve floors of offices, the base garden covers a third of an acre and a thirteen-foot level change. Temperate-zone plants, dominant, include the mighty southern magnolia. Above, gardens hang from the third, fourth, fifth, and eleventh floors.

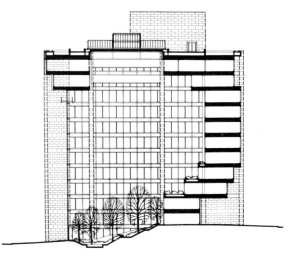

Zion & Breen: Paley Park, 3 East 53rd Street, New York, 1965–68.

New York's first vest-pocket park, this privately endowed haven for mid-town shoppers and workers is an outdoor room of remarkable civility. The vine-clad sidewalls—vertical lawns, Zion calls them—are those of adjacent buildings. Honey locusts branch out as light-dappling canopy and the cascade of the far water-wall submerges street noise. Contributing to one's peaceful pleasure are inexpensive refreshments and generous seating arrangements.

since 1964

Affleck Desbarats Dimakopoulos Lebensold Sise, architects (R. T. Affleck, partner-in-charge); Sasaki, Dawson, Demay Associates, landscape architects: Hotel Bonaventure, Montreal, 1962–67.

One would not guess that the garden inn pictured above crowns the formidable bulk of the Place Bonaventure and rests on an international trade center, five levels of Merchandise Mart, two levels of exhibition space, two levels of retail shops, and eighteen railroad tracks. The four hundred hotel rooms ranged along the periphery of the roof are separated by an inner ring of gardens from the public rooms at the center.

Earlier roof gardens, other than Le Corbusier's, seem afterthoughts when compared to this, carved into the mass of the building, and to those on the facing page.

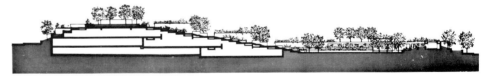

Kevin Roche and John Dinkeloo, architects; Dan Kiley, landscape architect: Oakland Museum, Oakland, California, 1961–69.

When the city decided to build a regional museum, it might have been tempted to counter Gertrude Stein's famous disparagement of Oakland ("There is no there there.") with a monument which would shout defiance to San Francisco across the bay.

Instead, the five-acre site, originally a park, was kept as a park—but now a park composed in large part of the roof gardens and terraces of the low, irregularly stepped pyramid that is the museum. Each gallery opens to terraces and the variously shaped outdoor spaces are connected by a network of paths and broad stairs. Over all this intricate, elusive geometry Kiley threw a lovely veil of greenery.

With these hanging gardens Oakland eloquently affirms its presence.

Lawrence Halprin & Associates: Portland Open Space Sequence, Portland, Oregon, 1961–68.

A walk to the central city through this redeveloped area is an adventure. Each of the three one-acre plazas alone would be a rare pleasure. Joined as they are by traffic-free footways, enjoyment is compounded by an artful ordering of sensuous and emotional response.

Halprin's understanding of the streams and cascades of the High Sierras is first evident in Lovejoy Plaza (right), where stepped "mountains" invite all comers to enter into the waterplay. Most likely drenched, one then proceeds to peaceful Pettigrove Park, a shady retreat where grassy mounds suggest privacy. Then on through the greenway to the thundering grandeur of the auditorium forecourt (below) with its abstraction, eighty feet wide, of a great natural waterfall. Running gently at first, water gathers force as it drops down the "cliffs" to crash into the pool. The rectangular slabs at the base pile up as though shoved by floods.

Neither this park sequence nor Philadelphia's (page 38) is in midtown, where continuity is more difficult to achieve.

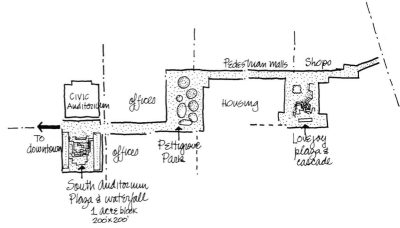

since 1964

Philip Johnson and John Burgee, architects; Zion & Breen, landscape consultants: Fort Worth Water Garden, Fort Worth, Texas, 1970–74.

Broad steps, straight-edged but irregular, transform the flat land into solid/void, mountain/water. Ascending, they are planted terraces; descending into the maelstrom, they are water-stairs for fearless Texans. Gift to the city of the Amon G. Carter Foundation, the Water Garden covers a full block near downtown Fort Worth.

Artificially contrived as they are, the running, falling waters of Fort Worth and Portland (pages 104–105) seem far more "natural" than yesterday's jets.

SWA Group/Sausalito, landscape architects (George Hargreaves, project designer); Gensler & Associates, architects: Harlequin Plaza, 7600 East Orchard Road, Greenwood Village, Englewood, Colorado, 1980–82.

As disorienting in actuality as in this photograph, the plaza defies the bleak ordinariness of Denver's suburban sprawl. Two low mirror-image, mirror-surfaced office buildings break for a court bisected by a swathe of harlequin-patterned pavement which points west to distant snow-capped Rocky Mountains. Mechanical elements of under-plaza garage and services erupt through the black-and-white terrazzo diamonds— boiler flue as skewed black tower, chiller (right foreground) as mirror-clad box. A high red wall tapers down as it runs west through the plaza to end below a converging purple wall. Rarely visible between them is a narrow watercourse embellished with jets which dwindle in height as they move west. Despite this forced perspective the mountains do not actively enter the scene. Nature is vividly engaged, but only as mirrored reflections of shifting clouds. Buildings and courtyard, inseparable, dissolve in ambiguity.

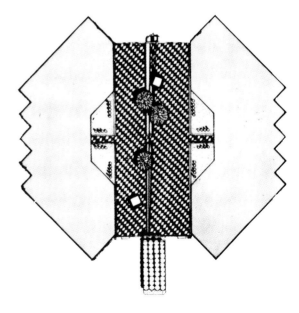

107

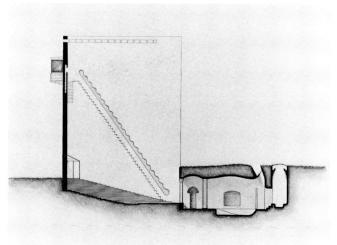

Emilio Ambasz: House near Cordoba, Spain, 1979–82. (Photographs of the completed building are not available.)

The sunken patio of this weekend retreat is defined on two sides by living quarters, on the other two sides by tall white walls. Living space runs cool beneath the rolling wheat-field to curving slits of light and air at the periphery. The tall walls at their juncture are punctured by a ground-level entrance from which steps fan down to the courtyard; and from the courtyard a narrow stair, water burbling in its scalloped handrail, runs up each white wall to a balcony perched high above the entrance and dedicated to meditation.

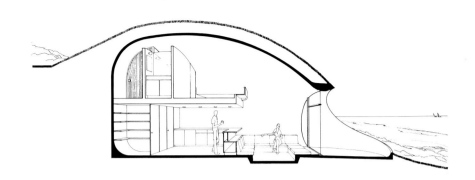

William Morgan: Dunehouse, Atlantic Beach, Florida, 1974–75.

Dunehouse presents mystery to beachcombers, just another sand dune to grateful neighbors, and duplex apartments to its two tenants. The eyes are terraces fronting glass-ended living rooms, and the building's curving concrete shell, unobtrusive in this setting, carries its heavy load of earth and plants more efficiently than the flat roof customary in modern earth shelters.

Energy conservation through built-in protection against extreme temperatures is of course the main reason for growing interest in earth shelters; but retreat into the ground, with or without earth cover, is an act of self-effacement with impact that can be social and spiritual as well as visual. (See also Soleri's Cosanti Foundation, page 57.)

LEFT. Gianni Avon, Francesco Tentori, and Marco Zanuso: New Cemetery, Longarone, Italy, 1969–73.

"Yea, though I walk through the valley of the shadow of death. . . ."

BELOW. Carlo Scarpa: Brion-Vega Cemetery, San Vito de Altivole, Treviso, Italy, 1970–72. (Illustrated in color on the back cover.)

This private cemetery, Scarpa's masterwork, celebrates the union of opposites—life/death, male/female, advance/retreat, fullness/emptiness.

The focal tomb is in plan a circle. Above is a canopy of vine-clad arches, their curves reflected in grassy steps. Ascending and descending arcs join heaven and earth.

Throughout the cemetery, steps are the persistent theme: steps for stepping on, steps that lose themselves in water, and above all, steps molded into the concrete of buttresses, beams, walls, roofs, entrances— advancing and receding in rhythmic counterplay that recalls such forgotten wisdom as one might ascribe to Assyria or pre-Columbian Mitla. These intricately stepped moldings might earn Frank Lloyd Wright's approval as "organic ornament."

index

photograph credits

In the preparation of this book we were dependent upon existing photographs. Work of great interest often had to be omitted for lack of convincing illustrations; on the other hand, some of the included work has been flattered by selective and expert photography. The aim, however, was less a compilation of "bests" than a bringing together of provocative pictures. To the photographers, professional and amateur, go my warm thanks.

—E. B. K.

Peter Aaron/ESTO: 98 top; Charles Agle: 28 top; Marinus Andersen: 47; *Architectural Forum*: 24 plan; Morley Baer: 42 bottom, 44, 69; Berko: 36 bottom, 56; Ernie Braun: 52 top; Hugo Bryan, courtesy USDA Soil Conservation Service: 14; Chicago Park District: 72, 73 left; Gerry Campbell/SWA Group: 107 top; John Cliett © Dia Art Foundation 1980: 97; Connecticut General Life Insurance Co.: 75 bottom; *Country Life*: 9 right, 10 right, 55; Creative Photo Service: 109 bottom; Richard Cripps: 46; Sylvia Crowe's *Garden Design*: 30; Dandelet: 89; Dell & Wainwright: 84 bottom; *Domus*: 60–61; Nicolau Drei: 92; Charles Eames: 53 bottom, 87; Carl Feiss: 88–89; Roy Flamm: 24, 25; Freer Gallery, courtesy National Palace & Central Museums, Taichung, Taiwan: 11; Marcel Gautherot: 37, 48, 62, 66, 67; Alexandre Georges: 58, 106 top; Gösta Glase: 19, 40 top; Heikki Havas: 85; Hedrich-Blessing: 90, 91; Lucien Hervé 23, 32 right, 81; David Hirsch: 99 bottom; George Holton: 27; Susan Jellicoe: 78; Henrique Mindlin's *Modern Architecture in Brazil*: 67 plan; Molitor: 64; Moulin Studios: 45; Nelson Gallery: 9 left; Joseph Nettis: 39 right; New York State Department of Public Works: 86 top; Paul Oreby: 31 bottom; Richard Payne: 106 bottom; Photochrome Ltd.: 10 left; George Pohl: 41; Armando Salas Portugal: 33, 34, 35, 50, 65, 70, 71, 86 bottom; Stephen Proehl: 103 top; Retoria/Yukio Futagawa: 110 bottom; Paul Ryan: 104; Tatsuzo Sato: 4 bottom; P. C. Scheier: 16; George Silk, courtesy *Life* Magazine © 1963 Time Inc.: 82 top; G. E. Kidder Smith: 28 bottom, 31 top, 77 bottom; Ezra Stoller: 20, 68 right, 73 right, 74, 75 top, 83, 93, 100 left; Stewart's: 54; Gene Stutz: 57 bottom; Swedish Tourist Traffic Association: 36 top, 76 left, 77 top, 79; Soichi Sunami: 59; Lou de la Torre: 95; *UIA International Architect*: 99 top; Anthony Walmsley: 53 top, 63; Lawrence S. Williams, Inc.: 39 left; Catherine Wurster: 12 right; Italo Zannier: 110 top; Zion & Breen: 101. COLOR PHOTOGRAPHY. Marcel Gautherot: between 48–49; Armando Salas Portugal: front cover, between 32–33, between 79–80 (bottom); Retoria/Yukio Futagawa: back cover; Julius Shulman: between 64–65; Ezra Stoller: between 79–80 (top).

112